What Kinship Is—And Is Not

What Kinship Is— And Is Not

MARSHALL SAHLINS

The University of Chicago Press ❀ Chicago and London

The University of Chicago Press, Chicago 60637
The University of Chicago Press, Ltd., London
© 2013 by The University of Chicago
All rights reserved. Published 2013.
Paperback edition 2014
Printed in the United States of America

23 22 21 20 19 18 17 16 15 14   3 4 5 6 7

ISBN-13: 978-0-226-92512-7 (cloth)
ISBN-13: 978-0-226-21429-0 (paper)
ISBN-13: 978-0-226-92513-4 (e-book)
DOI: 10.7208/chicago/9780226925134.001.0001

Library of Congress Cataloging-in-Publication Data
Sahlins, Marshall David, 1930–
    What kinship is—and is not / Marshall Sahlins.
        pages; cm
    Includes bibliographical references and index.
    ISBN 978-0-226-92512-7 (cloth: alkaline paper)—
    ISBN 0-226-92512-9 (cloth: alkaline paper)—
    ISBN 978-0-226-92513-4 (e-book)—
    ISBN 0-226-92513-7 (e-book)   1. Kinship.   I. Title.
    GN487.S25 2012
    306.83—dc23   2012013886

⊚ This paper meets the requirements of ANSI/NISO
z39.48-1992 (Permanence of Paper).

E. B. Tylor spoke with some wonder of "South American tribes who consciously believe that different persons are not necessarily separate beings, as we take them to be, but that there is such a physical connexion between father and son, that the diet of one affects the health of the other."
« E.B. TYLOR, *Researches into the Early History of Mankind and the Development of Civilisation* (1865) »

We become the children of our children, the sons of our sons. We watch our kids as if watching ourselves. We take on the burden of their victories and defeats. It is our privilege, our curse too. We get older and younger at the same time.
« COLIN MCCANN, "What Baseball Does to the Soul," *New York Times*, April 1, 2012 »

Contents

Preface

This small book amounts to a modest proposal for solving the 150-year-old anthropological problem of what kinship is. The specific quality of kinship, I argue, is "mutuality of being": kinfolk are persons who participate intrinsically in each other's existence; they are members of one another. "Mutuality of being" applies as well to the constitution of kinship by social construction as by procreation, even as it accounts for "the mysterious effectiveness of relationality," as Eduardo Viveiros de Castro put it, how it is that relatives emotionally and symbolically live each other's lives and die each other's deaths. Involving such transpersonal relations of being and experience, kinship takes its place in the same ontological regime as magic, gift exchange, sorcery, and witchcraft. But to thus know what is kinship is to imply as well what it isn't. If chapter 1 is devoted to the former question, "What Kinship Is—Culture," chapter 2 concerns "What Kinship Is Not—Biology." For even the relations of procreation already entail the greater kinship matrix whose social persons they produce. In contrast to our own native wisdom and an anthropological science that for too long has been indebted to it, kinship categories are not representations or metaphorical extensions of birth relations; if anything, birth is a metaphor of kinship relations.

>>><<<

Chapter 1 is a revised version of an article originally published (in two installments) in the *Journal of the Royal Anthropological Institute* (Sahlins 2011). I thank the editor, Matthew Engelke, for his encouragement and for allowing me that space, and the copy editor, Justin Dyer, for work at once well done and beyond the usual line of such duties. In acts of collegiality for which I am most grateful, a number of scholars read earlier drafts of the present text or parts thereof and offered their opinions, criticisms, and/or suggestions. Adopting the usual caveat that they are not responsible for any errors in the text (although they could be), I heartily thank for their comments: Maurice Bloch, Robert Brightman, Janet Carsten, Philippe Descola, Gillian Feeley-Harnik, Klaus Hamberger, Robert McKinley, Susan McKinnon, Anne-Christine Taylor, Thomas Trautmann, and Eduardo Viveiros de Castro. Special gratitude to Alan Rumsey for extended e-mail exchanges on several relevant issues. Originally, "What Kinship Is—Culture" was a lecture delivered at the University of Bergen in honor of Professor Bruce Kapferer's seventieth birthday. It is now over thirty years that Bruce has been a friend and an inspiration, as he continued to be in connection with this work.

1

What Kinship Is—Culture

The social universe [of Palau people] is divided into persons who are classed as *kauchad* 'mutual person(s)' and those who are simply *ta er tir* 'one of them.' . . . Ties of mutuality are commonly established through concepts of shared blood, shared land, shared exchange and/or shared ancestors who once behaved as 'mutual people.' . . . These ties of mutuality are glossed as 'kinship' by English-speaking Palauans. (Smith 1981, 226)

Native [Piro] communities focus on the relationships in which food is produced, circulated, and consumed, such that for native people, to live with kin is life itself. (Gow 1991, 119)

Despite the variation in and complexity of what [Korowai] kin relations are, it is worth postulating an overall quality by which these relations are known and measured. I will call it a quality of "intersubjective belonging." . . . [A] kinship other is a predicate of oneself. A speaker recognizes the other as the speaker's own, and embraces the other as an object proper to the speaker's own being. (Stasch 2009, 129, 132)

What is crucial in traditional Ashanti law, moral values, ritual practice, and personal sentiment is the notion that the *abusua* as lineage is "one person," *nipa koro*. This, again, is no metaphor. It is another way of expressing the fact . . . that a lineage is of "one blood," *mogya koro*, transmitted matrilineally from a single common ancestress. (Fortes 1969, 167)

The dala [clan of Gawa Islanders] forms the core of the individual's self. . . . [I]t grounds the bodily person in pre-given, transbodily being through bonds of bodily substance (notably by blood) to other, living and dead, persons. (Munn 1986, 27)

This is a Frazerian-style piece, which is to say, an exercise in uncontrolled comparison. As graduate students, we used to call the like an "among-the-text," with ethnographic examples cherry-picked from among this people and that. My defense is that I am not trying to prove empirically what kinship is, only to make some exposition of what I claim it is. I am trying to demonstrate an idea, for which purpose the ethnographic reports are mainly meant to exemplify rather than verify.

In brief, the idea of kinship in question is "mutuality of being": people who are intrinsic to one another's existence—thus "mutual person(s)," "life itself," "intersubjective belonging," "transbodily being," and the like. I argue that "mutuality of being" will cover the variety of ethnographically documented ways that kinship is locally constituted, whether by procreation, social construction, or some combination of these. Moreover, it will apply equally to interpersonal kinship relations, whether "consanguineal" or "affinal," as well as to group arrangements of descent. Finally, "mutuality of being" will logically motivate certain otherwise enigmatic effects of kinship bonds—of the kind often called "mystical"—whereby what one person does or suffers also happens to others. Like the biblical sins of the father that descend on the sons, where being is mutual, there experience is more than individual.

Constructivism

It seems fair to say that the current anthropological orthodoxy in kinship studies can be summed up in the proposition that any relationship constituted in terms of procreation, filiation, or descent can also be made postnatally or performatively by culturally appropriate action. Whatever is construed genealogically may also be constructed socially: an affirmation that can be demonstrated across the known range of societies and not infrequently within a given society (Bamford and Leach 2009; Carsten 2000a, 2000b, 2004; Franklin and McKinnon 2001; McKinnon 2006). Indeed, constructed forms of so-called "biological" relationships are often preferred to the latter, the way brothers by compact may be "closer" and more solidary than brothers by birth. But then, kinship is not given by birth as such, since human birth is not a pre-discursive fact. A whole series of persons may be bodily instantiated in the newborn child, including lineage and clan ancestors, while even the woman who gave birth is excluded— in which case, as Karen Middleton observes, "it becomes inappropriate to say either that 'women make babies,' or . . . that 'the mother-child *relation* in nature is plain to see'" (2000, 107; emphasis in original). This would be all the more so where parentage is formulated through the postnatal practice thereof, as among the To Pamona of Sulawesi:

> The ease with which children move from house to house reflects a notion of parentage rooted in nurturance and shared consumption rather than narrowly defined biological filiation. . . . It cannot be assumed that the recognition of "natural" parentage flows automatically from the event of birth. . . . To Pamona parents and children see the recognition of parentage as emergent through time and effort. (Schrauwers 1999, 311)

Symbolically formulated and culturally variable, human reproduction involves a differential valuation of the contributions of the genitor and genetrix that ranges to some sort of parthenogenesis—the woman functioning as medium only or the man's role unacknowledged—and at the limit, to the exclusion of both. Long ago, E. B. Tylor noted the doctrine of "the special parentage of the father," as in the Code of Manu where the mother is compared to a field that yields the plant of whatever seed is sown in it. Again in the *Eumenides* of Aeschylus, Tylor wrote, "the very plea of Orestes is that he is not kin to his mother Klytemnestra, and the gods decide that she who bears the child is but nurse to it" (1878, 299). Karla Poewe (1981) argues that the like is found in many patrilineal societies, the converse being the occasional indifference of a matrilineal people to the male contribution to conception, such as the so-called ignorance of paternity among Trobriand Islanders. What may not be depreciated, however, is the necessary participation of third parties such as ancestors, gods, dreamtime spirits, or the potency acquired from captured enemies. Maurice Godelier and Michel Panoff (1998, xvii–xviii), surveying this issue across a number of societies, conclude that two human beings are insufficient to produce another human being; the intervention of a spiritual third is also required.[1] Moreover, the world around, human begetters are connected to their offspring by a great variety of transmitted substances—blood, semen, milk, bone, genes, flesh, soul, etc.—with various effects on children's appearance and character. Although it is an axiom of our own native folklore that "blood" ties are "natural" and irrevocable, as David Schneider demonstrated in well-known studies of American kinship (1968, 1977, 1980), in truth, as he also told, they are as conventionally made as relatives by marriage. "Substance" is as constructed as "code"—for what is to be conveyed in procreation is not mere physical substance but social status.

For that matter, among Amazonians, a birth may involve no kinship ties with anyone, if what the woman bore was the child of an animal (Vilaça 2002). Certainly as regards shared substance, the Kamea of New Guinea are not the only ones who know no such connections between children and those who conceived them (Bamford 1998, 2007, 2009). Parenting is also devalued in the reincarnation concepts of many circumpolar societies. On the Alaska North Slope, the Iñupiat will name children and sometimes adults after dead persons, thus making them members of their namesakes' families. Over a lifetime, reports Bar-

---

1. The intervention of spiritual parties seems particularly true of descent-based kinship orders, where lineage or clan ancestors are necessary participants in conception. The ancestor is in effect the co-generator of the child; hence clanmates are effectively siblings, and rather than an "extension" of "primary" kin relationships, classificatory kinship is present from birth. This will be discussed further in chapter 2.

bara Bodenhorn (2000, 137), an Iñupiat may acquire four or five such names and families, although those who bestow the names were not necessarily related before, and in any case they are never the birth parents. Begetters, begone: natal bonds have virtually no determining force in Iñupiat kinship. Kinship statuses are not set by the begetters of persons but by their namers. Indeed, it is the child who chooses the characteristics of birth, including where he or she will be born and of what sex.

Among the far-off Greenland Inuit, when a child is named after a deceased relative—say, a maternal grandfather—he addresses his birth mother as "daughter," her husband as "daughter's husband," and his grandmother as "wife" (Nuttal 2000, 48–49). One is reminded of stock African examples of mothers' brothers who are called "male mother" (Radcliffe-Brown 1924) or wealthy Lovedu women who use their cattle to acquire "wives" and become "fathers" to the latter's children (Krige and Krige 1943). Inasmuch as brothers and sisters of the Karembola people (Madagascar) are of one kind, "rooted in one another"—n.b., the mutuality of being—a man can claim to have given birth to his sister's son: "I am his mother. He is my child. Born of my own belly. Made living by me. Crying for the breast" (Middleton 2000, 104). Thus men who are mothers, women who are fathers: there is nothing inevitable about the kinship of procreation.

It is not even inevitable that the kinship of procreation is essentially different from relationships created postnatally. Kinship fashioned sociologically may be the same in substance as kinship figured genealogically, made of the same stuff transmitted in procreation. For the New Guineans of the Nebilyer Valley studied by Francesca Merlan and Alan Rumsey, kinship, whether by sexual reproduction or social practice, is produced by the transmission of *kopong*, "grease" or "fat"—"the essential matter of living organisms, whose ultimate source is the soil" (1991, 42–45). Conveyed in the father's semen and mother's milk, *kopong* founds a substantial connection between a child and its birth parents. Yet as such "grease" is also present in sweet potatoes and pork, the same consubstantial effect can be achieved by food-sharing, commensality, or eating from the same land. In this way, the children or grandchildren of immigrants may be fully integrated as kinfolk; but for that matter, the offspring of two brothers are as much related because they were sustained by the same soil as because their fathers issued from the same parents.[2]

Elsewhere in the New Guinea Highlands, as reported of the Maring by Edward LiPuma, for example, the generative "grease" flows into the land from the bodies of clansmen and "from there (through the use of labor and magic) into taro, pigs and other foods, and then ultimately returns to clansmen through eating food" (1988, 6–7; see also Strathern 1973). Or as neatly put for Baruya by Maurice Godelier: "The land nourishes men, but men by their flesh fatten the land that they leave to their descendants" (1998, 10; the critical word is *engraisser*, to "fatten" or "fertilize," thus something of a trilingual pun). Similarly in New Caledonia: "The yam is a human thing. Since it was born in the earth in which the ancestors are decomposed . . . the yam is the flesh of the ancestors" (Leenhardt 1979, 62). Kinship thus produced from the fruits of the ancestral earth is summed up deftly by Clifford Sather in reference to the Iban of Kalimantan, for whom "rice is the transubstantiation of the ancestors" (1993, 130).

Thus the capacity of shared food to generate kinship—a mode of "consumptive production" that Marx did not imagine. Rather to the point, however, was Marx's notion of a tribal community that included the objective conditions of its existence as an extension of itself, from which it might well follow that the land has certain intersubjective relations with its human possessors, or indeed a certain kinship with the people (Marx 1973, 471ff.). Or perhaps John Locke's notion of men claiming ownership by mixing their labor with the land is more pertinent for its direct implication of mutuality of being. In South Pentecost, the effect of just such a transfer of being, reports Margaret Jolly, is that,

2. Thanks to Alan Rumsey for calling attention to this example.

"the human inhabitants merge with the land. Thus, like children, land is not so much owned as part of one's human substance" (1994, 59). Likewise, Jane Goodale on Kaulong people of New Britain, for whom all descendants of an ancestor are "'together brothers,' sharing similarity of biogenetic substance not only with each other but with a place and its resources" (1981, 280). In his excellent monograph *Creative Land,* James Leach details how Reite people of New Guinea's Rai Coast "incorporate places into bodies and bodies into places" (2003, iv). As against those who argue that kinship is an idiom or metaphor of land-holding (e.g., E. Leach 1961a), property supposedly being the utilitarian reality of the matter, James Leach shows that land and the persons integrated with it are in the same ontological register. The land and the people are alive and akin:

> The land is very much alive, and enters directly into the constitution (generation) of persons. The relation between land and person is not one of containment, with the land outside and the essence of the person inside, but one of integration. . . . [T]he constitution of persons and of places are mutually entailed aspects of the same process. In this sense kinship is geography, or landscape. (2003, 30–31)[3]

3. Descended from Papa, the Earth Mother, the Maori are not the only people for whom the land is the primordial ancestress. In Plato's *Menexenus*, Socrates claims to have overheard Aspasia, Pericles' mistress, composing the latter's famous funeral oration for the Athenians killed in the first year of the Peloponnesian War. Rehearsing a theme of Athenian autochthony, the dead soldiers were true "children of the soil," she said.

> And the country which brought them up is not like other countries, a stepmother to her children, but their own true mother; she bore them and nourished them and received them, and in her bosom they now repose. . . . And the great proof that she brought forth the common ancestor of us and of the departed is that she provided the means of support for her offspring. For as a woman proves her motherhood by giving milk to her young ones . . . so did this our land prove she was the mother of men, for in those days she alone and first of all brought forth wheat and barley for human food. . . . And these are truer proofs of motherhood in a country than in a woman, for the woman in her conception and generation is but the imitation of the earth and not the earth of the woman.

Then again, the social construction of kinship may function as a necessary complement of sexual reproduction, the two working together over time to forge a parental bond. Anne-Christine Taylor (2000) relates how the Amazonian Jivaro (Achuar) develop the kinship of father and son through a process that begins with the former's contribution of semen in sexual reproduction, continues with the food he provides during pregnancy, and is definitively achieved by his nourishment of the child in life. Note it is the nurture, rather than the transfer of bodily substance, that makes the relationship, for, by Jivaro lights, "procreation does not suppose a substantial connection between parent and child" (Taylor 2000, 319).[4] Moreover, unlike kinship by procreation alone, an extended temporality is a condition of the relatedness at issue, since it requires a cumulative process of parental care—a condition more or less true of many forms of performative kinship. It follows that memory is also essential, the recall of acts of compassion. "Memory for Amazonian peoples is essentially linked to kinship. Indeed, in some sense it is kinship itself" (Taylor 1996, 206). Likewise, Aparecida Vilaça writes of the Wari':

> It is not just substances which circulate. The Wari' body is also constituted by affects and memories. Memory, say the Wari', is located in the body, meaning the constitution of kin is based to a high degree on living alongside each other day-to-day and on reciprocally bestowed acts of affection. (2005, 449)

Given such possibilities of kin relationship—that is, on the basis of shared life conditions and shared memories—one can imagine why the constructed forms of kinship are legion. Ilongot of the Philippines say that those who share a history of migration and cooperation "share a body" (Rosaldo 1980, 9). The Malays studied by Janet Carsten acquire the same "blood" by living in the same house and eating from the same hearth, "even when

---

4. Margaret Mead (1935, 36) reported a similar practice for New Guinea Arapesh, where a father's parental claim is not that he has begotten the child but that he nourished it.

those who live together are not linked by ties of sexual procreation" (2004, 40). A catalogue of commonplace postnatal means of kinship formation would thus include commensality, sharing food, reincarnation, co-residence, shared memories, working together, blood brotherhood, adoption, friendship, shared suffering, and so on. But the performative modes of kinship known to anthropology—if not to sociobiology or evolutionary psychology—are indefinitely many, inasmuch as they are predicated on particular cultural logics of relatedness. In certain Inuit groups, people born on the same day are kin, even as those are "brothers" whose parents once had a sexual liaison, although they are no longer together and neither of the brothers was born of their union.

Indeed, the Eskimo-speaking peoples must be the world champions of postnatal kinship. Notoriously flexible as well as inventive, their kinship practices not only demonstrate that relationships of all kinds may be constructed in practice, but equally that they may be deconstructed in practice. As Mark Nuttal says of Greenlanders: "If a relationship does not exist, then one can be created. At the same time, people can deactivate kinship relationships if they regard them as unsatisfactory. People are therefore not constrained by a rigid consanguineal kinship, but can choose much of their universe of kin" (2000, 34). The people's freedom to revise their kin relationships, however, does not mean that the relationships as such are under revision—or otherwise without determinate properties and codes of conduct. In a highly performative kinship order, as that of the Inuit, the existing relations between persons are potentially unstable: continuously vulnerable to events and ever subject to negotiation. Unfortunately, such common instabilities of practice have likewise made kinship studies in anthropology vulnerable to the deconstructionist dispositions of the (former) avant-garde in cultural theory.

Privileging the "realities" of practice over the "essentialisms" of structure, a certain indulgence in what James Faubion called "the messy content of daily life" (2001, 1) threatens to leave kinship in that limbo of indeterminism where postmodernism habitually came to rest. Faubion says that because people "fudge," "make kin," "change kin," and "forge and consecrate alliances of greatly diverse sorts," an "older anthropology of kinship" has been forced "to endure the perturbations of an ever more unruly 'supplement' (a term that I use in its Derridean sense . . .)" (1). What the argument overlooks is that not all differences in practice are necessarily differences in form—let alone negations thereof—since identity itself is a selective determination of certain (culturally) relevant resemblances among the many possible ones. Only certain qualities are essential. Many differences in practice may be as insignificant for the integrity of kinship categories as variations in pronunciation are for the integrity of phonemes. Cecilia Busby makes this point nicely in discussing Dravidian kinship in India:

> However much one loves one's mother's brother, for example, and however much he acts like a father, he remains *categorically* different. The kinship system is categorical, while emotion and affect are individual and haphazard, and one cannot be explained in terms of the other. Not all brothers love their sisters (or even *like* them), yet all brothers *are* related to all sisters in a particular way. (Busby 1997, 29; emphases in original)

For similar categorical reasons, the contingencies of people's kinship choices should not be conflated with some disorder in the kinship they choose. Responding to this confusion in Inuit studies, Nuttal allows that while people often decide what kinship relationships are appropriate to them, they do not thereby decide what is appropriate to their relationships. He writes, "While the flexibility of the kinship system allows individuals to choose who they want to have as their relatives (or who they do not wish to have as a relative), it does not give them license to decide how they should behave with that person" (2000, 45; see also 35, 39). Inuit people are not the authors of the kinship relations they adopt, as indeed it is the already-existing meanings of these relations that make them desirable or not. Kinship is in this way the perduring condition of the possibility of its (unstable) practice.[5]

In this connection one may well ask, with Eduardo Viveiros de Castro (2009), whether the constructivist preoccupation with optation—since it singularly problematizes certain relations of consanguinity while assuming no such argument is necessary for the obviously "made" character of affinity—does not subtly perpetuate our own folkloric distinctions of "nature" and "law," "biogenetic substance" and "code for conduct"? What to make then of Amazonia, where the presupposed generic notion of kinship—applicable to other peoples, certain animal species, strangers, and even gods—is affinity, not consanguinity? Here virtually all men are brothers-in-law, actual or potential, rather than brothers. Yet if both consanguinity and affinity are constituted by human agency, still anthropologists have felt compelled to prove it only for consanguines. Fixed, moreover, on the biological attribute of bodily substance, this proof merely extends the sense of an organic connection from the sphere of the given to that of the constructed. Biology is still there, as Viveiros de Castro remarks, only it has less value than it had before, and sometimes less value than the socially constituted. It would seem that constructivism—although largely inspired by David Schneider's critique of the extension of our own biological fixations to the understanding of kinship in other societies—has nevertheless come too close to the same pass.

5. Not to rule out the risk of practice to kinship categories and the possibilities of change. By and large, change in kinship categories is beyond the scope of the present work. But I will say that something depends on just who is innovating, under what circumstances, and with what powers. Also, any such change in a category, however contingently motivated, enters into relations with coexisting categories as well as with the world; hence the effect, though it be altogether novel, is also likely to be a culturally relevant form (cf. Sahlins 2000; 2004, chap. 3; 2008).

Schneider and Durkheim

Or perhaps one should say, the same impasse. Schneider's discussion in "What Is Kinship All About?" (1972), and its subsequent elaborations (1977, 1980, 1984), is reminiscent of certain famous philosophical birds that glide in ever-decreasing hermeneutic circles until they fly up their own backsides. Long study of "kinship" had convinced him that there was no such thing. Neither at home nor abroad did "kinship" exist as a distinct cultural system, nor *a fortiori* as a comparative, cross-cultural category. Happily, this led to numerous and enlightening analyses of kinship the world around by anthropologists who were explicitly indebted to Schneider's work. It seems his announcement of the end of kinship had the logical force of the famous observation of the Cretan that "All Cretans are liars."

Schneider was trained in an era of social science hubris that from its center in the lesser Cambridge spread its Parsonian doctrine that any differences that could be "usefully" discerned in the object of anthropological study were legitimate analytic distinctions. Imitating the Galilean resoluto-compositive method, Parsons famously divided the social science world into a set of component "systems"—notably the social, the cultural, and the psychological—a division that by now seems as arbitrary as it was then influential, especially in its distinction between social structure and the cultural order. Even at the time, it struck some that the project was like analyzing water into its discernible elements of hydrogen and oxygen in order to understand why it runs downhill.[6] Just so, Schneider's critique of kinship began from an *a priori* radical differentiation of a "normative system" of

---

6. At the time, Clyde Kluckhohn made a relevant objection. As Adam Kuper describes it:

> Specifically, Kluckhohn objected that social structure should be treated, in part at least, as an element of culture: "social structure is part of the cultural map, the social system is built upon girders supplied by explicit and implicit culture." According to to Parsons, Kluckhohn was too much of a humanist to accept that social structure

of social actions and relations from a pure "cultural system" of symbols and meanings: as if the norms and relations of motherhood, cross-cousinship, brotherhood through eating from the same land, and the like were *not* constituted by and as "symbols and meanings." Following Paul Ricoeur in this regard, "we should have to say, according to this generalized function of the semiotic, not only that the symbolic function is social, but that social reality is fundamentally symbolic" (1979, 99).[7] Commenting on and also agreeing with this observation, Nancy Munn notes that "the practices by means of which selves construct their social world, and simultaneously their own selves and modes of being in the world, are thought to be symbolically constituted and themselves symbolic practices" (1986, 7). Since what Schneider meant by "culture" was nothing more nor less than ontology, what there is for any given people, it was inevitable that the "symbols and meanings" he discovered in "kinship" would not be exclusive to that domain. And since what he meant by the social or normative system were prescriptions of people's interactions, it was inevitable that these were ordered by "symbols and meanings." I quote at length:

> By symbols and meanings I mean the basic premises which a culture posits for life: what its units consist in; how these units are defined and differentiated; how they form an integrated order or classification; how the world is structured; in what parts it consists and on what premises it is conceived to exist. . . . Where the normative system, the how-to-do-it rules and regulations, is Ego-centered and particularly appropriate to decision-making or interaction models of analysis, culture is system-centered and appears to be more static and 'given' and far less processual. . . . Culture takes man's position *vis-à-vis* the world rather than *a* man's position on how to get along

---

could be separated from culture as "an authentically independent level in the organization of the components of action." (1999, 55)

7. Others—including Marcel Mauss and Lévi-Strauss—have made this argument about the symbolic nature of the social. See especially Leslie White's (1949) contentions in this vein against Radcliffe-Brown.

in the world as it is given; it asks, "Of what does this world consist?" where the normative level asks, "Given the world to be made up in the way it is, how does a man proceed to act in it?" (Schneider 1972, 38; emphasis in original)

Apparently Schneider did not notice that in distinguishing the cultural system from social action in the way the ontologically presupposed is to the humanly made, he produced as anthropological theory the functional equivalent of the contrast between naturally given relations of "blood" and the made relations of "in-laws" he had discovered in the American kinship system. Insofar as the ontological is the natural within the cultural itself, as also are "blood" relations, one may even speak of permutations of the same "symbols and meanings." Nor did Schneider refer this kinship contrast of "biology" and "code for conduct" to the opposition of *physis* and *nomos*, nature and law (or nature and convention), that has been inscribed in Western ontology since it was elaborated by Greek sophists in the fifth century BC (Dillon and Gergel 2003; Kahn 1994; Sahlins 2008). And whereas a structuralist would be pleased to find fractal repetitions of the same opposition—most notoriously, the opposition of nature and convention (i.e., culture)—in various registers of cultural practice, for Schneider the parallels of the kinship contrast of nature and code in the Native American concepts of "nationalism" and again "religion" were proof that there was no such cultural thing as a "kinship system." Why this should be so has never been very clear, since it does not follow that because kinship shares certain ontological characteristics with nationalism and religion, it therefore has no specific properties of its own. Nor has anyone (so far as I know) called out Schneider on his curious reduction of "nationalism" to the way citizens are recruited, whether by birth or naturalization, or the equally tendentious resolution of "religion" to how membership is established in church or synagogue (1977, 69–70). This is hardly what these cultural "units consist in; how these units are defined and differentiated," and so on. Schneider should be credited, however, with taking the argument to its logical conclusion, for he deduces from the similarities between American kinship and his bargain definitions of nationalism and religion that there is no such thing as "nationalism" or "religion" either, culturally speaking (1972, 59).[8]

A. M. Hocart called the Fijian kinship system "a whole theology" (1970, 237). "Sacred blood" (*dra tabu*) flowed from the paternal house with an out-marrying woman, to become manifest in the divine privileges of the uterine nephew (*vasu*), the woman's son. In ritually appropriating the sacrifices offered by his mother's brother's people, this privileged nephew not only usurped their god, but also established enduring relations of material aid and political alliance between his own and his maternal kin (Hocart 1915; Sahlins 2004). Adding the many corollary details would show that Fijian kinship, without losing its determinate character but rather because of it, is also a whole economy and a whole politics. In the typical traditions of dynastic origins, the Fijian paramount chief, a stranger by paternal ancestry, is the sister's son of the indigenous people—whence come intimations of his divinity and specifications of his authority (Sahlins 1981, 2004).

Culture, as Marilyn Strathern has put it, "consists in the way people draw analogies between different domains of their worlds" (1992, 47). The method Schneider used to deconstruct a culture is now the normal science of cultural order. This goes some way toward explaining the paradoxical impetus that his writing against kinship gave to the cross-cultural study of it. Positioning kinship in the realm of "symbols and meanings," Schneider introduced a productive "cultural turn" to a field that had gone meaningless and sterile, largely by its obsession with jural rights and obligations, and more generally by the paralyzing theoretical effects of the culture-social structure distinction.

8. Indeed, by the logic of Schneider's argument, there would be no such thing as anything: no possible internal differentiations of a cultural order, inasmuch as a shared ontology obviates all such distinctions of register or domain.

Yet even as many ethnographers were parlaying his insights into important works on the diverse cultural forms and values of kinship relations, Schneider held to the answer of his article, "What Is Kinship All About?"—namely, "in the pure cultural level there is no such thing as kinship" (1972, 50). "From the beginning of this paper," he wrote, "I have put the word 'kinship' in quotes, in order to affirm that it is a theoretical notion in the mind of the anthropologist which has no discernible cultural referent in fact" (50). Or again:

> If "kinship" is studied at the cultural level . . . then it is apparent that "kinship" is an artifact of the anthropologist's analytic apparatus and has no concrete counterpart in the cultures of any of the societies we studied. Hence the conclusion that "kinship," like totemism, the matrilineal complex and matriarchy, is a non-subject, since it does not exist in any culture known to man. (59)

But as I say, Schneider's own project was based on an ontological distinction without a difference, for it is only by ignoring the symbolic constitution of social relations that one can speak of "the irreducibility of the cultural to the social systems, or vice versa" (60). It is some testimony to the fateful outcome of this Parsonian problematic that Hildred and Clifford Geertz, who were likewise schooled in it, also came to doubt "that kinship forms a definable object of study to be found in a recognizable form everywhere, a contained universe of internally organized relationships awaiting only an anthropologist to explore it" (1975, 153).

In sum, studying phenomena that do not exist by the ethnocentric means of our own *physis/nomos* dualism, now all anthropologists would be liars.

Including Émile Durkheim, whom Schneider put in the company of L. H. Morgan and followers in attributing kinship to the natural facts of biological reproduction. Of course, Durkheim did employ the opposition of nature and culture in his sociology: most importantly in his notion of duplex man, whose egocentric, presocial dispositions were sublimated by social constraints; and rather in passing (in the *Elementary Forms*) by the argument that collective representations are to social structure as the ideational is to the natural. But Durkheim's notions of kinship were thoroughly and explicitly constructionist. So much so that to pin some sort of genealogical fallacy on him would require a wholly conjectural stretch, which Schneider manages to achieve by certain unsupported allegations to the effect that the French master's sociological explications entailed a covert biologism:

> Durkheim implicitly depended on some motivating factor, some hidden motor behind kinship to make it work. That motor was probably biology in the form of the axiom that Blood Is Thicker Than Water. But it had to be kept implicit, as motivation was kept implicit while he focused on the social facts, on kinship as social relations. (Schneider 1984, 191)

Actually the key text, noted at length by Schneider, is Durkheim's radical constructivist critique of a book by J. Kohler on the history of marriage that, for its part, defended Morgan's derivation of kinship from the knowable conditions of procreation (Durkheim 1898). Published in the inaugural volume of *L'Année Sociologique*, Durkheim's review is still cited today by those who likewise claim that "kinship organization expresses something completely different than genealogical relations," that it "essentially consists in juridical and moral relations sanctioned by society," and that it "is a social tie or it is nothing" (Durkheim 1898, 318). Obviously, this unequivocal differentiation of kinship from consanguinity and genealogy was sequitur to Durkheim's central project of disengaging the social as an autonomous phenomenal realm, subject only to its own determinations. As a social fact, kinship had to be explained by other social facts rather than reduced to biology or psychology. Hence Durkheim's sustained demonstration of the disconformity between kinship values and genealogical proximity; his notices of the creation of kinship by adoption and ceremonial legitimation, and its abolition by emancipation (in Roman law); and his detailed argument that Omaha and Choctaw kinship vocabularies "must express something completely different from the relations of consanguinity strictly speaking" (315). If in Omaha the same term is applied to mother, mother's sister, mother's father's sister, mother's brother's daughter, and mother's brother's son's daughter, we are not dealing with practices of marriage and procreation. So what are we dealing with?

According to Schneider, Durkheim does not tell us "what kinship is all about" (1984, 101), since the claim that it consists of moral and juridical relations will not distinguish it from other social relations. This is certainly true in the sense that Durkheim offered no explicit intensional definition of kinship. Yet in regard to certain aspects of its social nature, he did make a point of its distinctive quality, "some hidden motor behind kinship to make it work" (to adopt Schneider's expression). In the course of arguing for the independence of kinship from genealogy, he offered a determinate sense of what kinship is: mutual relations of being, participation in one another's existence. The point appears first in connection with the evident disproportions between the value of certain kinsmen—for example, as matrilineally or patrilineally related—and degrees of genealogical proximity. Some particularity of religious belief or social structure could make a child more closely or distantly attached to its mother than its father, Durkheim said, "more intimately mixed [*melé*] in the life of one or the other, so that it will not be the relative of the one or the other to the same degree" (1898, 317). Second, the same is implied by totemism, which for Durkheim was a primitive condition of familial relations, and

> if such is the case, to be a member of a family it is necessary and sufficient that *one have in oneself something of the totemic being*. . . . But if this *participation* can result from reproduction (generation), it can also be obtained in many other ways: by tattooing, by all forms of alimentary communion, by blood contract, etc. (317; my emphasis)

Durkheim did not know it, but what sweeter confirmation of his sociology of kinship could there be than the derivation of the English and French scholarly term "totem" from a Proto-Algonquian word for "co-resident"—via the Ojibway *do.de.m* "patrilineal clan," "clan eponym"?[9]

Mutuality of Being

In his capacity as a missionary, Maurice Leenhardt once suggested to a New Caledonian elder that Christianity had introduced the notion of spirit (*esprit*) into Canaque thought. "Spirit? Bah!" the old man objected: "You didn't bring us the spirit. We already knew the spirit existed. We have always acted in accord with the spirit. What you've brought us is the body" (1979, 164). Commenting on this interchange, Roger Bastide wrote, "The Melanesian did not conceive himself otherwise than a node of participations; he was outside more than he was inside himself" (1973, 33). That is, Bastide explained, the man was in his lineage and his totem, in nature and in the *socius*. By contrast, the missionaries would teach him to sunder himself from these alterities in order to discover his true identity, an identity marked by the limits of his body.

Later in the same essay, Bastide transposed this Melanesian sense of personhood to the African subjects he was principally concerned with, and in so doing produced a clear description of the "dividual person," the one destined for anthropological fame from the writings of McKim Marriott (1976) and Marilyn Strathern (1988). Bastide wrote of the person "who is divisible" and also "not distinct" in the sense that aspects of the self are variously distributed among others, as are others in oneself. Emphasizing these transcendent dimensions of the individual, he noted that "the plurality of the constituent elements of the person" moved him to "participate in other realities." Reincarnating

9. Thanks to Rob Brightman for this etymological comment on totemism.

an ancestor, he had a portion of the lineage within him; associated with a totem, he had an "exterior soul" as well as an internal one; knowing a bush-dwelling twin, he overcomes the distance that separates him from sacred space. Hence for the African as for the Melanesian, "he does not exist except in the measure he is 'outside' and 'different' than himself" (Bastide 1973, 38).[10]

This, then, is what I take a "kinship system" to be: a manifold of intersubjective participations, which is also to say, a network of mutualities of being. The present discussion thus joins a tradition that stretches back from Strathern, Marriott, and Bastide; through Leenhardt, Lévy-Bruhl, and Durkheim; to certain passages of Aristotle on the distinctive friendship of kinship. The classical text is the *Nicomachean Ethics*. Anchored as it may be in concepts of birth and descent, Aristotle's discussion of kinship at once goes beyond and encompasses relations of procreation in larger meanings of mutual belonging that could just as well accommodate the various performative modes of relatedness. Or so I read the possibilities of his sense of kinship as "the same entity in discrete subjects":

> Parents love children as being themselves (for those sprung from them are as it were other selves of theirs, resulting from the separation), children [love] parents as being what they have grown from, and brothers [love] each other by virtue of their having grown from the same sources: for the selfsameness of their relation to *those* produces the same with each other (hence the way people say "same blood," "same root," and things like that). They are, then, the same entity in a way, even though in discrete subjects. . . . The belonging

10. Among other early ethnographic notices of "dividuals," there is Nancy Munn on Gawan funeral custom:

> Gawan mortuary practices are concerned with factoring out the marital, paternal and maternal components which have been amalgamated to form the deceased's holistic being, and with returning this being to a partial, detotalized state—its unamalgamated matrilineal source. Death itself . . . dissolves neither the intersubjective amalgam that constitutes the *bodily person* and forms the ground of each self, nor the intersubjective connections between others built on and condensed within the deceased's person. (1986, 164; my emphasis)

to each other of cousins and other relatives derives from these, since it exists by virtue of their being of the same origins, but some of these belong more closely while others are more distant, depending on whether the ancestral common sources are near or further off. (Aristotle 2002, VIII.1161ᵃ–1162ᵇ; emphasis in original)

Of course, as the sage says, such intersubjectivity comes in various forms and degrees. But generally considered, kinsmen are persons who belong to one another, who are parts of one another, who are co-present in each other, whose lives are joined and interdependent. Ethnography tells repeatedly of such co-presence of kinsmen and the corollaries thereof in the transpersonal unities of bodies, feelings, and experience. Before exploring the relevant notion of being and its entailments, however, it is useful to consider a few examples.

Such as the ancient comment on kinship from the eastern side of the Indo-European world that effectively rehearses the kinship unities of common descent discussed by Aristotle: "The notion of basic similarity between those engendered by the same male is beautifully underlined in the *Panduan*, a localised Himalayan version of the *Mahabharata* when Arjuna referring to Bhima says, 'I am his brother, his cousin, his offspring, as also his ancestor'" (Böck and Rao 2000, 7).

In *The Maori and His Religion* (a yet-to-be-acknowledged classic of kinship studies), J. Prytz Johansen writes: "Kinship is more than what to us is community and solidarity. The common will which conditions the solidarity is rooted in something deeper, an inner solidarity of souls" (1954, 34). Johansen cites an old text collected by John White: "'You were born in me,' says a Maori. 'Yes that is true,' admits the other, 'I was born in you.'" The interchange of being is more complex here than it appears, Johansen notes, if due to the same sense of transpersonal existence, for the Maori pronoun "I" is also used to refer to one's entire kinship group (*hapuu*, usually), past or present, collectively or in regard to famous members. More on this "kinship I" in a moment, but in the present connection recall the distinctive possessive pronouns in Polynesian languages that notably refer to certain relatives and parts of one's body, and signify an inalienable and intrinsic attachment. A similarly telling semantics of common being is conveyed by the pronouns affixed to kinship terms in New Caledonia, thereby making the possessed person appear "an integral part of the possessor" (Leenhardt 1979, 13).

Something similar is also involved in the difference reported for English townspeople by Jeanette Edwards and Marilyn Strathern between relating to others and "being related." As they write, "The belonging produced by kinship has, for these people, a whole further dimension to it" (2000, 153). Persons in Alltown may have a sense of common belonging through what belongs to them, but "families consider themselves as people who belong to one another" (150). Janet Carsten develops a similar conclusion from contemporary accounts of adopted persons who search for their birth kin. Without knowledge of their birth mother, though to a lesser extent the father, these people, Carsten comments, apparently experience a sense of self as "fractured and partial." Here, then, is a notion of personhood where kinship is not simply added to bounded individuality, but where "relatives are perceived as intrinsic to the self" (2004, 106–7).

Just as English families are "people who belong to one another," so for the Nyakyusa of the African Rift Valley, kinsmen are "members of one another" (Wilson 1957, 226). Monica Wilson puts the phrase in quotation marks, although it is unclear whether she is citing Nyakyusa rather than St. Paul on the relations between members of the body of Christ. Like the constructivism of the latter, however, Nyakyusa conceive a kinship of mutual being with co-residents of their age-villages as well as consanguines and those to whom cattle have been given, that is, affines (Wilson 1950, 1951). Inversely if to similar effect, Victor Turner relates of the Ndembu that people live together because they are matrilineally related, for "the dogma of kinship asserts that matrilineal kin participate in one another's existence" (1957, 129). All this gives sense to Wilson's useful characterization of kinship terms as "categories of belonging," a phrase also adopted

by Bodenhorn in regard to Iñupiat (2000, 131). Kin terms indicate kinds and/or degrees of conjoint being: their reciprocals
thus complete a relationship that amounts to a unity of differentiated parts (see below). Brothers and sisters, say Karembola
people of Madagascar, are "one people"; they are "people of one
kind"; they "own one another" (Middleton 2000, 113).

Defining kinship in regard to the Korowai people of Western New Guinea as "inter-subjective belonging," Rupert Stasch
(2009, 107, 129ff.) provides a superb ethnography of the argument I make here. People's possessive prefixing of kinship terms,
Stasch writes, "emphasizes that a kinship other is a predicate
of oneself. A speaker recognizes the other as the speaker's own,
and embraces that other as an object proper to the speaker's own
being" (132). In some respect, his discussion is even useful for a
certain ambiguity, in that he rather stresses "belonging" in the
differentiating sense of "possession," thus implying a self/other
relation, while noting also the alternate sense of "being a part
of," thus of mutual co-presence (132).[11] However, when discussing the subjectivity of kin relationships, the emotional and moral
solidarity, there is no doubt he is speaking of "mutuality of being"
in the latter meaning, for he uses that very phrase:

> Reckoning with ways that emotion, value, and morality are integral
> to kin categorization, anthropologists have often previously linked
> kin relationships to feelings of intersubjective mutuality of being,
> using such terms as "conviviality," "love," "care," "amity," and "en-
> during, diffuse solidarity." . . . These vocabularies are all pertinent
> to understanding Korowai kin relatedness. Korowai themselves fre-
> quently describe specific kin relations in terms of a feeling of "love,
> longing, care" (*finop*) for a person, a mental activity of "caring for,

11. The self/other opposition is reiterated in Stasch's adoption of Faubion's observation that "the terms of kinship are inherently linking terms; . . . they render the self in
and through its relation to certain others (and vice versa)" (Faubion 2001, 3; quoted in
Stasch 2009, 132). In the work referred to, Faubion treats kinship as a technology of the
self in the Foucauldian sense: a technology of "subjectivation" consisting in part of "sub-
jection" (or Althusserian "interpellation") and in part of self-fashioning (2001, 11ff.).

loving" (*xul duo*–; lit., "thinking about") another person, or a moral position of being "unitary, solidary, amicable" (*lelip*; lit., "together") with someone. (133)

Stasch here refers to a number of well-known observations on kinship amity, including those of Schneider (1968, 1984), Meyer Fortes (1969), and Robert McKinley (2001). Just as well known are the reservations almost all anthropologists quickly append, so soon as they speak of kinship love, to the effect that in practice not all kin are lovable—and often the closest relatives have the worst quarrels (see below). In Stasch's own terms: "Kinship belonging is an impossible standard: the ideal includes its own failure" (2009, 136). No gainsaying that, but that does not gainsay either the amity subsumed in kinship relations of interdependent existence. I take diffuse enduring solidarity and the like as the corollary subjectivity of mutual being. Aloha is even implied, although of course love is not a relation of kinship alone and no matter that it is honored in the breach. A breach of kinship love also implies the constituted love of kinfolk: the failure includes its own ideal.

We are inevitably led to Marilyn Strathern's discussion of the "dividual" Melanesian person, a text that has inspired so many other ethnographic discoveries of the like, and not only in Melanesia. In Strathern's oft-quoted characterization:

> Far from being regarded as unique entities, Melanesian persons are as dividually as they are individually conceived. They contain generalized sociality within. Indeed, persons are frequently constructed as the plural and composite site of the relationships that produced them. The singular person can be imagined as a social microcosm. (1988, 13)[12]

---

12. Alan Rumsey (personal communication) points out that, according to this characterization, Melanesian persons are as individually as they are dividually conceived—which poses something of an unexamined problem. Probably Strathern meant a dividual person as an individual entity (or subject).

Beside her own experience in the New Guinea Highlands and her readings of other Melanesian societies, Strathern's description of the person as the "composite site" of the substances and actions of plural others has resonated in ethnographic reports from around the region, including Vanuatu (Hess 2009, 51ff.), Fiji (Becker 1995, 4), Tanga (Foster 1990, 432), and the Trobriands (Mosko 2010). Then again, the same "dividual" has been found in Polynesia (Mosko 1992) and Micronesia (Lieber 1990, 74), as well as Ming China (Clunas 2004, 11) and the New Kingdom Period of ancient Egypt (Meskell and Joyce 2003, 17–18)— not to forget McKim Marriott's (1976, 111) original exposition of the "dividual" in South Asia and Bastide's (1973) *avant la lettre* discussion of the "African person." To adopt the title of a currently popular American television series, *Curb Your Enthusiasm*: the Strathernian "dividual" is threatening to become a universal form of premodern subjectivity. Some of this generalization of the concept would indeed be warranted, insofar as the reference is to kinship domains. But a good part, I believe, follows from a certain confusion between personhood and kinship relations, with its corollary conflation of partibility and participation. Persons may have various relational attributes and thus be linked to diverse others—the way I am related to my students as a teacher and to the Chicago Cubs as a fan—without being united in being with them.

But the issue here is kinship, and therefore a more sociocentric view of what is theoretically at stake than the makeup of individual persons. At least as much attention needs to be given to the transpersonal distribution of the self among multiple others as to the inscription of multiple others in the one subject, for what is in question is the character of the relationships rather than the nature of the person. Since Strathern was drawing a contrast to the autonomous Western individual—which in any case does not describe such individuals in their own family and kindred contexts—the effect was a highlighted interest in the "singular person" too much like the demarcation and celebration of the bourgeois subject that she was putting in question:

dividual individuals, as it were. Hence in her extraordinary work
The Gender of the Gift, there is a certain unresolved tension between the marked emphasis on dividual persons and the rela-
tively backgrounded relationships that constitute them—the intersubjective relationships that are taken here as the fundamental
elements of kinship order.

Considering the parallels in other ethnographic works, it seems
that there is a certain anthropological logic to a critique of Western individualism that leads to notions of the composite person.
I say "anthropological logic" because the "dividual" is not merely
a negation of the individual as we know him—especially him,
not so much her—but has a content that precisely involves the
participatory sense of kinship relations. Thus Deborah Gewertz
writes in an article on the Tchambuli (aka Chambri) that is expressly concerned, as indicated in the subtitle, with a "critique of
individualism in the works of Mead and Chodorow":

> Tchambuli describe a patriclan as "the people with the same totems,"
> a phrase that indicates that members of the clan hold common own-
> ership of numerous totemic names—names referring to the ances-
> tors who once held them and to the territories and resources owned
> and lived in by these ancestors. . . . Each individual also inherits
> several totemic names from his or her father's affines. Thus, Tcham-
> buli become repositories of both their patrilineal and matrilineal re-
> lationships through their possession of certain names. To be a person
> among them is to embody these relationships. (1984, 619)

Note not only the embodiment of relationships in the person,
but the synthesis of being through name-sharing such as we already saw among Inuit (and will have other occasions to remark
upon). For another even more general contrast to the bounded
and self-regarding bourgeois individual that explicitly entails
the mutual beingness of kinship, consider the broad argument
penned by Julian Pitt-Rivers:

> . . . the majority of the world's peoples do *not* share the individualism
> of the modern West and have no need to explain what appears to

them evident: the self is not the individual self alone, but includes, according to circumstances, those with whom the self is conceived as solidary, in the first place, his kin. (1973, 90; emphasis in original)

For all that "the person" is a current idol of the anthropological tribe, as an analytic category it may itself derive some motivation from the hegemonic force of bourgeois individualism. That helps explain why the partible "dividual" has become a regular figure of kinship studies as well as an icon of the premodern subject. It appears that we have been staring for too long at ego-centered-*cum*-egocentric, kinship diagrams. The problem here is not just the category mistake of rendering the relationships of kinship as the attributes of singular persons. The problem is that kin persons are not the only kind who are multiple, divisible, and relationally constructed. In this connection, not enough attention has been paid to Alan Rumsey's (2000) demonstration—following Émile Benveniste (1971) and Greg Urban (1989) on the meaning and use of personal pronouns—that the capacities of partibility and hierarchy (or the encompassment of others) are general conditions of humans in language. "Moments of both encompassment and partibility are inherent in language," Rumsey writes, "corresponding to two distinct dimensions in which the pronouns are meaningful (the 'direct indexical' and 'anaphoric')" (2000, 101). Using Polynesian as well as Melanesian examples, Rumsey shows how in a single discourse the shifting frames of reference of the pronoun "I" can refer alternately to the current (partible) speaker, the collective kin group to which he belongs, or the long-dead chief who heroically instantiates the group. Of course, this does not mean these capacities are necessarily enacted in social practice, as in the modes of "dividual" persons and the "kinship I." Then again, as a general condition of possibility, partible and relational identities may characterize persons who are not "dividual" kin persons—but perhaps even bourgeois individuals like us.

Even individuals like us may be "employees," "clients," "teammates," "classmates," "guests," "customers," "aliens," and the like.

These are relational terms. When aspects of the same person, alternately salient in different social contexts, they are instances of partibility. But they are not instances of "dividuality"; since they do not entail the incorporation of others in the one person, making her or him a composite being in a participatory sense. Partibility thus describes a larger class of persons than "dividuality," which is a differentiated subclass consisting of partibility plus co-presence. The two should not be confused, although as personhood and kinship they often are. Perhaps this is how we get "dividuals" in the New Kingdom of Egypt—even as we might ignore that bourgeois persons are in their intimate kin relationships as "dividual" as Melanesians.

Not only should kinship and person be disentangled, but for understanding kinship, much is gained by privileging intersubjective being over the singular person as the composite site of multiple others. For one, the extensional aspects of kin relationships, the transpersonal practices of coexistence from sharing to mourning, are better motivated by the sociocentric considerations of mutuality. "Intrinsic" to each other, as Janet Carsten (2004, 107) put it, kinsmen are people who live each other's lives and die each other's deaths. To the extent they lead common lives, they partake of each other's sufferings and joys, sharing one another's experiences even as they take responsibility for and feel the effects of each other's acts. For another thing, mutuality of being has the virtue of describing the various means by which kinship may be constituted, whether natally or postnatally, from pure "biology" to pure performance, and any combinations thereof. In this connection, "being" encompasses and goes beyond the notions of common substance, however such consubstantiality is locally defined and established. Neither a universal nor an essential condition of kinship, common substance is better understood as a culturally relative hypostasis of common being. Then again, as the distinctive quality of kinship, mutuality of existence helps account for how procreation and performance may be alternate forms of it. The constructed modes of kinship are like those predicated on birth precisely as they involve the transmission of life-capacities among persons. If love and nurture, giving food or partaking in it together, working together, living from the same land, mutual aid, sharing the fortunes of migration and residence, as well as adoption and marriage, are so many grounds of kinship, they all know with procreation the meaning of participating in one another's life. I take the risk: all means of constituting kinship are in essence the same.[13]

Nancy Munn relates how a Gawa man begins to create a fosterage relation with an infant by premasticating food and putting it in the baby's mouth. "This transaction," she writes, "is a paradigmatic instance of food-giving as the separation of food from one's own body for incorporation by another" (1986, 50)—a description, note, that could serve as well for breast-feeding or pregnancy. Gift-giving, especially of food, is life-giving, as Johansen lays out at length for Maori. "Food can give a new nature since it can introduce a new kind of life into the eater. . . . The eater is not only bound to the givers, but they on the other hand recognize their own life in the guest who has eaten and respect this" (1954, 108). Moreover, the life-giving is normally reciprocal. Johansen goes on to explain how the life force in the gift compels a return from within the recipient, which is why Maori proverbially say, "Property is knitted brows." Although he is critical of Marcel Mauss's famous essay on the gift, Johansen essentially confirms that the *hau* of the gift is the why of the gift.

At the other extreme from common practices of gift exchange, some of the more idiosyncratic forms of postnatal kinship recorded by anthropologists are nevertheless motivated by comparable principles of shared existence—for example, the Trukese category "my sibling from the same canoe," referring to those who sustained each other through a life-threatening trial at sea. As described by Mac Marshall:

13. Hence like Roy Wagner, I take the view that "kin relationships are basically alike in some important way. . . . I might as well speak of one essential kin relationship, which is encompassed and varied in all the particular kinds of relationships that human beings discern and differentiate" (1977, 623).

This term refers to men who shared a disabled canoe, drifted aim-
lessly together at sea for many days supporting each other's flagging
spirits, and sharing completely what meager food and water they had
until they finally reached land or were rescued at sea. Born of mutual
aid in adversity these men swear eternally to treat each other like
brothers: they would . . . "take care of or look after one another," . . .
"cooperate," . . . "agree to be of one mind," and possibly . . . "share
land or other resources." These phrases encapsulate the essence of
proper kinship feeling. . . . (1977, 647)

Similar experiences may lead Greenland Inuit to form a name-
sharing kinship, even when they do not share a name: "They
choose to become name-sharers and address each other as *atîit-
sara* ["name-sake"] usually on the basis of a shared experience,
such as surviving a difficult time on the sea ice during a winter
hunting trip" (Nuttal 2000, 49; see also 52).

The same mutuality of existence is involved in trans-specific
relations of kinship, such as the plants who are children of the
Amazonian or New Caledonian women who cultivate them, or
the animals of Siberia and Amazonia who are affines of the men
who hunt them. This is no metaphor, but a sociology of moral,
ritual, and practical conduct. For Maori, kinship is cosmologi-
cal inasmuch as all things—including plants, animals, and "the
very elements"—descend from the same Sky Father (Rangi) and
Earth Mother (Papa). In the words of surveyor and ethnographer Elsdon Best:

> When the Maori entered a forest he felt that he was among his own
> kindred, for had not trees and man a common origin, both being
> offspring of Tane? Hence he was among his own folk as it were, and
> that forest possessed a *tapu* life principle even as man does. Thus,
> when the Maori wished to fell a tree wherefrom to fashion a canoe
> or house timbers . . . he was compelled to perform a placatory rite
> ere he could slay one of the offspring of Tane. (1924, 452)

The relevant Maori category of common belonging, *tupuna*—
normally translated as "ancestor" or "grandfather"—is classifi-

catory, denoting an ancient with some legendary significance for current life. Johansen (1954, 148) observes that in traditional sagas, *tupuna* may refer to flies, whales, birds, trees, the canoe that brought a tribe to New Zealand, and Captain Cook (for example). All such beings—including what we deem inanimate "things"—are subjects who share essential attributes of common descent, kinship, and personhood with Maori people.

Being and Participation

E. B. Tylor in his *Researches into the Early History of Mankind* of 1865 was probably the first to take anthropological notice of intersubjective being, complete with its contrast to European individualism, its presence in certain kin relationships, and its effects in transmitting the experience of one person to the existence of another. Not that Tylor was critical of his own native individualism. On the contrary, he considered the curious "psychology of the savage" a kind of ontological scandal, a confusion of "subjective connexions" with "objective connexions," although at the same time clearly worthy of wonderment. The context was primarily the "remarkable custom" of the couvade, especially the South American ritual practices in which the father apparently facilitates and imitates the labors of his wife in childbirth, and secondarily certain funerary ceremonies. The couvade finds an intelligible explanation, he wrote, "among South American tribes who consciously believe that different persons are not necessarily separate beings, as we take them to be, but that there is such a physical connexion between father and son, that the diet of one affects the health of the other" (1865, 369). We will come again upon this ability of one person to eat (or refrain from eating) for another, as also its basis in mutual being, which Tylor described as the deliberate opinion held by "a number of tribes"

that the connexion between father and child is not only, as we think, a mere relation of parentage, affection, duty, but that their very

bodies are joined by a physical bond, so that what is done to the one
acts directly upon the other. . . . Not only is it held that the actions
of the father, and the food that he eats, influence his child both
before and after its birth, but that the actions and food of survivors
affect the spirits of the dead on their journey to their home in the
after life. (292)

I realize that in speaking of "being," let alone "transpersonal
being," I risk dragging the discussion of kinship into dark philosophical waters, an epistemic murk made the more obscure by
an outmoded anthropological concept of "participation." Referring usually to independent entities, philosophical notions
of being have a common tendency to devolve into notions of
"substance," even as "substance" conjures a sense of materiality.
Hence mutuality of being—insofar as "being" carries such con-
notations—would be an inadequate determination of kinship.
For as argued here, "being" in a kinship sense denies the necessary independence of the entities so related, as well as the necessary substantiality and physicality of the relationship. To the
contrary, the being-ness of humans is not confined to singular
persons. Moreover, the most famous determination of the reality
of the *human* being—the *cogito ergo sum*—precisely by virtue of
(symbolic) thinking, is radically opposed to merely material substance (*res extensa*). The same symbolic capacity is pregnant with
the possibility of the mutuality of being: as, for instance, in the
interchangeability of persons and standpoints in the pronouns
"I" and "you" as well as other shifters (Benveniste 1971, chap. 20).
In your response to me, I become "you" and you become "I." This
synthesis of being in symbolic communication helps explain how
for some peoples, such as the New Guinea Korowai, merely in-
teracting in conversation can be a sufficient condition for the
adoption of kinship terms among strangers, since this is "a form
of mutuality of being and calls for a degree of such mutuality"
(Stasch 2009, 137). Given such mutuality, I for one have no res-
ervation about according the practice the status of kinship rather

than mere metaphor, it being both sociologically and symbolically kinship in essence.[14]

To be clear, I am not referring to the constitution of identity as a dialectical or mirrored reflex of the self configured from the way others know one (as in line of Hegel, G. H. Mead, Lacan, et al.). This is too much like a commodity notion of exchange in which each party appropriates what the other puts on offer; and in any case, the transaction presumes and maintains the separation of the persons so related, the opposition of self and other. Kinship entails an internalization of the difference even as it objectifies it: "an inner solidarity of souls," as Johansen (1954) says of Maori; children as the "other selves" of their parents, as Aristotle put it.

When in retrospect Lévy-Bruhl (1949) rid his problematic notion of "participation" of its dross of "pre-logical mentality," there remained the gold of his sense of shared existence that denied the classical oppositions between the one and the many and the one and the two (or the self and the other) (cf. Leenhardt 1949; Lévy-Bruhl 1949, 1985). "Facts of bi-presence" (*des faits de bi-presence*) are among the phrases he used in tortuously trying to describe the thing; also a "dual unity" as opposed to a "unified duality." Commenting on Lévy-Bruhl's late notebooks (in which his own observations figure prominently), Maurice Leenhardt said that if "participation" seems irreconcilable with the norms of our intelligence, it is because we take it for granted that beings are given beforehand and afterward participate in this or that relation; whereas, for Lévy-Bruhl, participations are already necessary for beings to be given and exist. "Participation is not a fusion of beings who lose or retain their identity at the same

14. For human-being-ness, consider the following Cartesian *bon mot* now making the philosophical rounds:

"I think, therefore I am," said Descartes.
I also think.
Therefore, I am Descartes.

time," said Lévy-Bruhl; "it enters into the very constitution of
these beings. It is immanent in the individual, a condition of
existence" (in Leenhardt 1949, xvi).

Just so, in his own Melanesian work, Leenhardt describes interpersonal kin relationships in terms of dual unities, as notably
evident in the "dual substantives" by which New Caledonians
and Fijians speak of paired relatives as in effect one personage.
The duality of subjects is conjugated into a higher-order, singular being:

> This substantive plays a special role in classic kinship relations
> where a single term joins the parties of grandfather and grandson,
> uncle and nephew, aunt and nephew, and the dualities of mother and
> child, father and male of the lineage. . . . The Canaque . . . retains not
> one or the other of the two personages, but a third one, known by
> the noun assigned to it. This third personage constitutes an entity:
> uterine uncle and nephew or grandfather and grandson, which our
> eyes obstinately see as two, but which form a homogeneous whole
> in the Canaque's eyes. (1979, 98)[15]

In a fundamental way, Lévy-Bruhl's synthesis of Plato's co-
nundrum of the one and the many by "participation" epitomizes
kinship notions of common descent and the lineages, clans, and
other groups so constituted. Here especially is the "one entity in
discrete subjects" of Aristotle. And conversely, the one subject
in discrete entities: the ancestor in his or her descendants. In
defining a class intensionally by a founding individual, the latter conjunction of the one and the many also reverses the usual
taxonomy of type and token, class and instance. Named as "Descendants of So-and-So" (*Ngai X, Ngati Y,* etc.), the members of
Maori tribal groups are not only identified by their ancestors but
themselves characterized by the latter's legendary idiosyncrasies

---

15. Of the relation of uterine uncle and nephew of the Gnau people (Sepik), Gilbert
Lewis says, "I believe they think of it as a kind of a whole or entity or thing" (1980,
197).

of behavior, appearance, speech, and the like.[16] Yet an even more striking expression of the unity of the person and the group, the one and the many, is what Johansen describes under the heading of the "kinship I": the use of "I," the first-person pronoun, by current tribal members to refer to the group as a whole, to narrate its collective history, and to recount the feats of ancestors long dead as their own doings—even as they may speak of tribal lands as personal possessions. Johansen explains:

> It is this kinship I which reveals itself in the rich traditions of the Maori: the history of the kinship group is his own. It is the kinship I which remembers old insults and old friendship; which sticks to its country and fights for it and which observes the customs of the ancestors, everything because it is the same unbroken I, which lives in all of it. (1954, 37)

And he exemplifies:

> A chief of part of the *Ngatiwhatua* tribe tells a piece of old tribal history as follows: "According to our knowledge the reason why the Ngatiwhatua came to Kaipara was a murder committed by the Ngatikahumateika. This tribe murdered my ancestor, Taureka. . . . My home was Muriwhenua. . . . Later I left Muriwhenua because of this murder. Then I tried to avenge myself and Hokianga's people were defeated and I took possession of the old country." (36)

All these events, comments Johansen, "took place long before the narrator was born" (36).[17]

---

16. Here is another suggestion, of which there are many more in chapter 2, that extensive kinship connections are already present in procreation doctrine rather than generalized from the so-called "primary" relationships of birth.

17. Johansen cites a pertinent passage from Elsdon Best:

> In studying the customs of the Maori, it is well to ever bear in mind that a native so thoroughly identifies himself with his tribe that he is ever employing the first personal pronoun. In mentioning a fight that occurred possibly ten generations ago he will say: "I defeated the enemy there," mentioning the name of the [enemy] tribe. In like manner he will carelessly indicate ten thousand acres of land with a

Similar forms of the "kinship I" have been reported for Fiji, New Guinea, Central Africa, and Northwest America. Franz Boas recorded the like from a Kwakiutl noble boasting of the marital and feasting feats of his great-grandfather, the ancestor of his house (*numaym*):

> Therefore I am known by all the tribes all over the world, and only the chief my ancestor gave away property in a great feast, and therefore they try to imitate me. They try to imitate the chief, my grandfather, who was the root of my family. (1921, 842–43)

To my knowledge, however, nowhere is the collective "I" as richly analyzed as in Johansen's text. I single out only one other aspect—his triple identification of kinship, fellowship, and *mana*:

> We have seen . . . that kinsfolk are to honour (*manaki*) each other because in this way they are attached to each other and realize the fellowship unity. . . . This *manaki* means "to create *mana*, fellowship"; to *manaki* is to give out of one's own life. (1954, 91)

Johansen repeatedly describes the "kinship I" as "fellowship," clearly in the *OED* sense of "participation, sharing (in an action, condition, etc.); something in common; community of interest, sentiment, nature, etc." "The 'I' which lives through the ages," he writes, "the kinship I, is the fellowship in contrast to the individual life" (1954, 149). Johansen thus anticipates Viveiros de Castro's extraordinary synthesis of kinship, magic, and gift exchange in Amerindian cosmologies: that is, as so many modalities of participatory influence (see below). Johansen similarly conceives *mana* as the politico-religious technique of fellowship, the active participation of one being with another. Because of his privileged connection to ancestral being, the Maori chief has more fellowship, more *mana*, and more occasion for the "kinship

---

wave of his hand, and remark: "This is my land." He would never suspect that any person would take it that he was the sole owner of such land, nor would any one but a European make such an error. (Best 1924, 1:397–98)

I" than others. Power is in this regard a certain unbalance of mutual being, which is also to say of genealogical priority.[18]

Parenthesis on Human Nature

Parenthetically, there is an interesting correspondence between the intersubjective participation under discussion here and the unique ability of human infants—as discovered in recent years—to synthesize the distinction of self and other in interactively created common projects that involve shared interests, perspectives, and goals. "Shared intentionality" is what Michael Tomasello and colleagues call it—or alternatively, "we-ness" and "we-intentionality"—on the basis of numerous experiments with very young children and non-human primates. The implication is quite like the conjugation of two into one as just discussed.[19] Summarizing an impressive body of complementary research in different fields going back to the 1970s, Colwyn Trevarthen and Kenneth Aitken (2001) describe essentially the same capacity under the terms of "innate intersubjectivity," "mutual-self-and-other-consciousness," "cooperative awareness," "companionship," and the like—"companionship" getting close enough to "kinship" to warrant this digression.

Even before they demonstrate linguistic competence, infants of twelve to fourteen months engage in communicative interactions involving role reversals, turn-taking, and dialogical corrective helping, in order to establish the shared mental constitution of the situation that will allow them to coordinate their actions

18. When I first did fieldwork in Moala, Fiji, I drank kava from a coconut cup later used by the governing chief of the island. Soon after he developed a painful abscessed tooth. When he had recovered and we drank kava together again, he made sure to give me a new cup. He had apparently attributed his misfortune to using my kava cup, supposing I had a privileged relation to our common ancestry. "We are all descended from Adam and Eve," he explained.

19. For general discussions of these researches and their anthropological implications, see Tomasello (1999a, 1999b, 2008, 2009); Tomasello, Kruger, and Ratner (1993); and Tomasello, Carpenter, Call, and Moll (2005).

toward a common objective—which may even be invisible. Also involved is a capacity for identification with the other that enables children to embed the content of another's perspective in their own—that is, to know the other's intentions and attentions—in a process that requires filtering out the irrelevant empirical aspects of the context of action. In the latter connection, apes do not point, as Tomasello (2006) has observed, certainly not in declarative and informative ways for the benefit of other apes—although young children do (Tomasello 2008, 123ff.). (One is reminded of the intellectual difficulties by Wittgenstein's famous observations on ostension: "Point to the color of something. How did you do that?") Also according to Tomasello's reading, the motives underlying these distinctive human skills are "helping" and "sharing." Clearly he does not mean the kinds of "altruism" and "reciprocity" that merely correlate and sustain the differences between self and other—if they are not designed to foster one's own interests, as sociobiologists perversely have it. Something of the opposite: in events of shared intentionality, the differences between individuals are resolved into a dual unity, a transcendent sociological condition of collectivity. Here altruism is but "a bit player . . . the star is mutualism" (Tomasello 2009, 52). Everything thus happens in shared intentionality as it does in kinship. By all counts, we are talking of the same thing.[20]

Trevarthen and Aitken are particularly concerned to document the earlier stages of this mutualism, important aspects of which they find in neonatal and even prenatal mother-child interaction. So they speak of a "protoconversational" activity present from birth, as manifest in the "imitations and provocations of newborns in close reciprocal interactions with adults who are seeking to make their behaviors interesting for, and contingent

20. In their involuted attempts to liken subhuman primates to humans by commonalities of reciprocity and altruism (so-called), sociobiologists rather miss the point. The point is that humans subsume self and other in a single collective entity, a "we-ness," which apes cannot do. In the terms of this book, they are not our "closest relatives"—one more evidence that kinship is not genealogy.

with the infant's signs of attending" (2001, 7).[21] As early as two
months, infants and mothers, through looking and listening
in turn, "were mutually regulating one another's interests and
feelings in intricate, rhythmic patterns, exchanging multimodal
signals and imitations of vocal, facial, and gestural expression."
"Just before the end of the first year, there was a rather sudden
development of joint interest of mother and infant in their sur-
roundings, triggered by the infant's emerging curiosity about the
timing and direction and focus of attentions and intentions of
the mother" (5). By age one, then,

> a baby can not only communicate with human expression without
> language, but can also energetically share complex arbitrary experi-
> ences boldly displaying to familiar persons an individual, socially
> adapted personality. . . . Motivation to regulate fluent person-to-
> person awareness, joint attention, and mutually adjusted intention-
> ality, all at once, is coming to the fore at this age. (6)

Similarly, Tomasello notes that at around nine months of age,
infants begin displaying "a whole new suite of social behaviors,
based on their ability to understand others as intentional and
rational agents like the self and ability to participate with others in interactions involving joint goals, intentions, and attention
(shared intentionality)" (2008, 139). With apologies to Rimbaud,
this shared intentionality is rather like *"Je est un autre"* to the second power; for in the process of interchanging standpoints, each
person, knowing the other to be an intentional being like himself
or herself, assumes the perspective of the other while knowing
the other is doing the same. By this ability to know another as

21. Here as elsewhere, Trevarthen makes a point of a mutuality that is more and
other than the instrumentalist, pragmatic, and referential views that dominate empirical
work in child development: "This active involvement [of the newborn] in communication of rudimentary intentions and feelings confirms that the human mind is, from the
start, motivated not only to elicit, guide, and learn from maternal physical care to benefit regulation of the infant's internal biological states, but also for cooperative psychological learning—the mastery of socially or interpersonally contrived meaning specified
in intelligent reciprocal social engagements" (Trevarthen and Aitken 2001, 6).

oneself and oneself as another, humans establish that transcendent tertium quid that is "the common ground necessary for cooperative communication" (Tomasello 2008, 126). They are able to comprehend the social situation from "a bird's eye view with the joint goal and complementary roles in a single representational act" (Tomasello 2009, 68). Here, then, is "a whole new world of intersubjectively shared reality":

> I have hypothesized that the fundamental social-cognitive ability that underlies human culture is the individual human being's ability and tendency to identify with other human beings. This capacity is a part of the unique biological inheritance of the species *Homo sapiens*. . . . Given infants' identification with others, experiencing their own intentionality in this new way leads nine-month-olds to the understanding that other persons are intentional agents, like me. . . . [Thereupon] a whole new world of intersubjectively shared reality begins to open up. (Tomasello 1999a, 90–91; see also Tomasello et al. 2005)

Consider the parallels to these experimental findings in Marilyn Strathern's report of the socialization of children in the New Guinea Highlands:

> The mind (will, awareness), I was told in Hagen, first becomes visible when a child shows feeling for those related to it and comes to appreciate the interdependence or reciprocity that characterizes social relationships . . . for example when the child acknowledges that its mother needs sticks for the fire quite as much as the child needs food to eat. A gloss of mutuality is put upon the unequal, asymmetrical relationship. (1988, 90)

Chimpanzees don't do these things. Evidently, they do not reflexively understand themselves as intentional agents nor do they understand and integrate their being with conspecifics on analogy to their own agency. Unlike humans, they "seem to lack the motivations and skills for the most basic forms of sharing psychological states" (Tomasello et al. 2005, 685). In experiments designed to test for shared intentionality, chimpanzees were apparently unable to reverse roles and thus make a common existence with a partner. They appear incapable, too, of referential acts such as the kind of pointing that intends that the other not merely orient bodily toward some perceptible object, but mentally toward a non-sensory objective or even toward an absent entity—which children of twelve to fourteen months can do (Tomasello 2008). Translating such findings in Kantian terms, one might say that apes lack certain *a priori*s of human experience, notably the sense of objective causality in many ways entailed in shared intentionality. They operate on solipsistic judgments of perception—"when the sun shines on the stone it grows warm"—rather than the "objective validity" of human empirical judgments—"the sun warms the stone" (Kant 1950, 49n et passim). Or again as Tomasello has it, failing to view the world in terms of "intermediate and often hidden forces"—which would *ipso facto* imply a symbolic faculty—they do not understand it "in intentional and causal terms" (1999a, 19; see also Tomasello, Kruger, and Ratner 1993).

Apes do evidently understand what others are doing, and they can prudently do the same, in which sense they "cooperate"—for their own reasons.[22] But they lack the ability to symbolically participate in others' existence and thus communalize their own. Reporting on a series of experiments designed to show whether

---

22. Tomasello comments on reports of chimpanzees' cooperation:

The most complex cooperative activity of chimpanzees is group hunting, in which two or more males seem to play different roles in corralling a monkey. . . . But in analyses of the sequential unfolding of participant behavior over time in these hunts, many observers have characterized this activity as essentially identical to the group hunting of other social mammals such as lions and wolves. . . . Although it is a complex social activity, as it develops over time each individual simply assesses the state of the chase at each moment and decides what is best for it to do. There is nothing that would be called collaboration in the narrow sense of joint intentions and attention based on coordinated plans. . . . There are no published experimental studies—and several unpublished negative results (two of them ours)—in which chimpanzees collaborate by playing different and complementary roles in an activity. (2006, 521)

chimpanzee behavior could be mutually beneficial, selfish, altruistic, or spiteful, the experimenters concluded: "The main result across all studies was that chimpanzees made their choices solely on personal gain, with no regard for the outcomes of a conspecific" (Jensen et al. 2006, 1013). It follows that *only apes have human nature*:

> Traditional models of economic decision-making assume that people are self-interested rational maximizers. Empirical research has demonstrated, however, that people will take into account the interest of others and are sensitive to norms of cooperation and fairness. [This is probably because the "people" involved are already co-members of a specific society, not tabula rasa "human beings" as assumed in certain psychological and economics experiments.] In one of the most robust tests of this finding, the ultimatum game, individuals will reject a proposed division of a monetary windfall, at a cost to themselves, if they presume it is unfair. Here we show that in an ultimatum game, humans' closest living relatives, chimpanzees (*Pan troglodytes*), are rational maximizers and are not sensitive to fairness. These results support the hypothesis that other-regarding preferences and aversion to inequitable outcomes, which play key roles in human social organization, distinguish us from our closest living relatives. (Jensen, Call, and Tomasello 2007, 107; see also Jensen et al. 2006)

So much, then, for the dismal economic science—whose future is not bright either, inasmuch as chimpanzees are disappearing.

It seems rather more than coincidence that in the same way as anthropologists discovered the intersubjectivity of being in kin relationships, the experimental researchers who discovered the innate mutualism of human infantile behavior did so in opposition to the prevailing instrumentalism and individualism of their science. In fact, much of the recent scientific attention to the intersubjective capacities of the very young remains skeptical—which is not surprising, "given the individualistic, constructivist, and cognitive theory in empirical psychology" (Trevarthen and Aitken 2001, 3). In empirical psychology, including research in neuropsychology and psychiatry, the singular concern has been the functioning of the individual mind. "The subject's or patient's self, often an unhappy and subjectively challenged one, remains the privileged unit, and most of his or her attributes are accounted for in mechanistic terms related to the cognitive processing of stimuli, regulations of cognitive effort and efficiency, or the neurochemistry of self-regulating emotions" (18). But lurking, then, in the researches of Trevarthen, Tomasello, and others is a veritable cultural revolution, with the unique human capacity for intersubjective solidarity in the vanguard, which would send the old ethnocentric regime of bourgeois individualism to the dustbin of superseded paradigms.

Finally, would not the egocentric anthropology of kinship share the same fate? What is the implication for anthropological science if mutuality of being is at once an inherent disposition of human sociality and the distinctive quality of kinship relations? It would not be that kinship as known in various societies is innately constituted, however, inasmuch as it is always culturally structured. Everything will depend on what is locally defined as "belonging to one another" by one or another criterion of the kind previously described—together with the necessary complement of what is different and excluded. In this regard, it comes as no surprise that a generic symbolic capacity is natural to humans, appearing in infants even before its expression in language and the acquisition of cultural order. It is just such expression that will order the human symbolic potential in various cultural ways, no one of which is the only one possible. Kinship could very well be an inherent human possibility, something like Roy Wagner's (1977) notion of an "analogic flow" of relationship. And if so, the usual supposition that kinship categories are generalizations of so-called "primary" relations of birth, or extensions of an abstract Ego's familial relations, will have to be turned around. Kinship rather would be formed by differentiation of the field of communicable others–*cum*–sociological similars: as by the institution of the incest tabu, in the way Lévi-Strauss (1969) famously argued, and Wagner similarly. Or as St. Augustine deduced from our common ancestry in Adam, the human world would have begun in kinship, only to have the pertinent relations filtered out in the social-symbolic process. In this view, the work of language and culture is to delimit and differentiate the human disposition for transpersonal being into determinate kinship relations by specific criteria of mutual being: having the same name, eating from the same land, born from the same woman, and so on. Kinship may be a universal possibility in nature, but by the same symbolic token as codified in language and custom, it is always a cultural particularity. Still, in many societies known to anthropology, kin relationships encompass everyone with whom one has peaceful dealings—including the anthropologist. And from all that has been said about the dialogic intersubjectivity of infants, we can understand how, for the Korowai people of New Guinea, just having a conversation with a stranger is enough to establish a kinship relation (Stasch 2009, 137). End of parenthesis.

Transpersonal Praxis

Mutuality of being will not only cover the range of ways kinship is constituted, from common substances to common sufferings, but it provides the logico-meaningful motivation for a wide variety of practices distinctive of people so related. It is the intelligibility in common ethnographic reports of the diffusion among kin of agency and material interest, of ritual participation in birthing and dying, and of the effects of bodily injury. The same sense of conjoined existence is involved in taking responsibility for the wrongful acts of relatives, for their fortunes in the hunt or war, even for the shape and health of their bodies. In sum, where being is mutual, experience itself is transpersonal: it is not simply or exclusively an individual function.

If kinsmen are members of one another, then in the manner and to the extent they are so, experience is diffused among them. Not in the sense of direct sensation, of course, but at the level of meaning: of what it is that happens, which is the human and discursive mode of experience, and as such capable of communicating the appropriate feelings and consequences to others. More or less solidary in their being, kinsmen accordingly know each other's doings and sufferings as their own. The old-time Maori Te Rangiheata "was a very competent man in that kind of matter," relates J. Prytz Johansen, "misfortunes of relatives were not concealed to him. . . . Others were less competent; but no doubt everybody had a possibility of immediately feeling what had happened to his kinsmen" (1954, 35). Maurice Bloch tellingly makes the point in connection with descent and domestic groups on a wide ethnographic scale:

> Many African and Asian peoples say that members of a descent group share the same bones. To say this is not to use a metaphor for closeness; it means exactly what it says in that these people believe that the bones of their body are part of a greater undifferentiated totality. In cases such as these the body is not experienced as finally bounded by the air around it; it is also continuous with parts of the bodies of people who in modern western ideology could be seen as 'others.' . . . What such *bodyness* implies is that what happens to other members of your household is, to a certain extent, also happening to you . . . (1992, 75; emphasis in original)

The specificity of the bones aside, Bloch's generalization can be supported from ethnographic reports from many parts—let alone what happens to "you" (the reader) in your own families. For one example, Anne Becker's fine description of the sociality of experience in Fiji, which she also finds widely distributed in Oceania. Here, "as in many other Oceanic societies, self-experience is intimately grounded in its relational context, in kin and village community" (1995, 5). Citing Leenhardt, Becker writes: "The traditional Melanesian's self-awareness was as a set of relationships. Experience was diffused among persons, not considered specific to the individual until contacts with the Western world, which imparted the notion of 'the circumspection of the physical being'" (5). Just so, in Fiji, "bodily information transcends exclusively personal experience and awareness and infiltrates the collective by relocating in other bodies and in the cosmos" (85). "Mystical interdependence," Monica Wilson called this, in connection with the communication of the effects of personal conduct among Nyakyusa kin. "From the point of view of kinship and marriage," she wrote, "the essential fact is that relatives are believed to be mystically affected by the very fact of their relationship" (1950, 126). A son who does not participate in the death rituals for his father can go mad; a uterine nephew who fails to drink medicines at the birth of twins to his maternal uncle may see his own children swell up and die (126). Understood as a meaningful sequitur to the condition of intersubjective being, such "mystical influences" account for a variety of widely distributed cultural practices that indeed defy the Western common sense of physical causes and bounded individuals.

For example, mourning customs that signify the mutuality of the bereaved kin and the dead. Death is shared among kinsmen, in one or more of several ways. For one, rituals that radically separate close relatives from the dead lest they disappear with them (e.g., Yanomami). For another, endocannibalism: the consumption of parts of the deceased by their close kin, who by this literal consubstantiality defy the death (e.g., Fore of New Guinea). Most common are mourning practices that signify a mutual death: that is, dying with one's kinsmen by self-mutilation, tearing one's clothing, going unwashed, not working, and other such forms of withdrawal from normal sociality. Sooner or later, however, the mourning is terminated, along with intimate connection with the dead. Nyakyusa testimonies of such practices collected by Godfrey Wilson also testify directly to the participation of the living in the being and death of their relative (in M. Wilson 1957, 37ff.). Indeed, people's kinship with the dead is here coterminous with their continued participation in the posthumous existence of the latter: when they are finally ritually separated from the deceased, the relationship is said to be at an end—although the shade will later be reincorporated in the kin group to effect its reproduction.[23] (A nice demonstration, that, of kinship as mutuality of being.) A well-informed Nyakyusa elder, speaks of certain mortuary practices:

> We go to bathe wearing leaves, we throw them away, we bathe, then we come back and shave our hair. This means we are driving away the shade (*unsyuka*), for at first he is in our bodies. . . . That [i.e., another ritual gesture] is to drive him away, to tell him: "Do not return to these your relatives here, you were in their bodies, now you are separate, we have driven you away, you are no relative of ours!" All that we do in the house there means that he is in our bodies and we are going to cast him out. The flour on the shoulder is like the flour paste in the hair, this is the corpse, we throw it away. (Wilson 1957, 50, 53)

On Gawa Island, rites of participation with and separation from the dead are respectively undertaken by affines and people of the deceased's own matriclan (Munn 1986, 164ff.). Painted black, their heads shaven, dressed in rough garb, the affines are "identified with the other (a dead spouse, a brother's child, etc. of another clan) in their own bodies." They are seen by the deceased's own clan as "having taken care of the deceased—as having their identities embedded in the deceased's being, and the deceased having been partially identified with them." Thus taking on the negative state produced by the death, the affines will eventually allow the deceased's own people to ritually reclaim him or her for the self of the clan. Hence in contrast to the affines' merging with the dead, for the clanspeople "an aspect of the self becomes temporarily separated in the other." In Munn's fine analysis, however, the play of being is even more complex, as among other aspects, she notes that in taking on the death, the affines "become means by which the deceased's dala [clan] observe their own grief and loss (their own dead person) objectified

---

23. See the discussion of the participation of lineage and clan ancestors in procreation in chapter 2.

outside them in the other. They are, as it were, witnesses of their own deathlike state" (167). Brilliantly told by the ethnographer, such are the various ways that variously related kinfolk die each other's deaths.

The Toraja of Sulawesi also knew both separation and continuity: rites for preventing souls of close relatives from joining the soul of the dead; and tabus on working their fields, offering hospitality, shouting or quarrelling (thus being heard by others), and like negations of their own social existence. In explaining the latter practices as smoothing the path of the deceased to the underworld, a Toraja elder drew a parallel to another custom of quite different kind but similar import:

> When we went out to fight, the women who stayed behind did all sorts of things by which they made it easier for men on the warpath and supported them. In the same way, we observe the mourning customs to help the soul of the dead person so that it will not have a bad time of it and will have a happy trip to the underworld. (Downs 1956, 84)

The "dual unity" of spouses, their immanence in one another, is evidently the common cause of many such accounts of the prescriptions and prohibitions placed on women when their husbands are engaged in vital pursuits outside the community. Separated in kinship origins by the incest tabu yet intensely joined by sexuality, the mutuality of connubium is especially fraught, combining as it thus does the potentialities of alterity and solidarity. Besides warfare, marked constraints on their wives' conduct may be in effect during men's trading expeditions, big-game hunting, deep-sea fishing, vision quests, and the like. In a certain way, the practice parallels marriage itself in conjoining beings external to the fellowship of one or the other spouse to bring forth new life. Motivated by concrete logics of analogy, the women's behavior usually entails some combination of imitations of their husband's success and abstentions to prevent misfortune. In this regard, tabus on women's sexual activity are commonplace, perhaps precisely because such liaisons would cut their husbands from the existing affinal powers of vitality and mortality—the "metaphysical influence" of affines, as Edmund Leach (1961b, 21) put it, which is the logical corollary of the reproductive gains and losses in spouse-taking and spouse-giving. A sometimes variant of the warfare tabus consists of the unwelcome effects on husbands of women's failures to respect the appropriate conduct when they are in a dangerous state—notably when shedding menstrual blood, which is itself a sign of failed reproduction (non-pregnancy). Marilyn Strathern writes of Hageners: "A husband cannot observe his wife's menstrual magic; he knows she has performed it through the appearance of his skin" (1988, 147). Well known in this connection, and in many respects a direct inversion of the behavior enjoined on women when their menfolk are warring, is the couvade: where the husbands, by imitation and abstention, sustain their wives when they are birthing even as they demonstrate their own connection to the child and their affinal kin (cf. Rival 1998). As recorded by Jane Atkinson, the Wana of Sulawesi go all out in such respects: men are said to menstruate, become pregnant, and give birth in the same way as women, if not as effectively (in Carsten 2004, 69).[24]

Also made intelligible by their mutuality of being is the way that sins of the father descend on sons, daughters, and other kinsmen, who then must suffer the effects. The effects may not extend to the seventh generation, but in the case of Nyakyusa, for example, they run at least to the great-grandchildren, who fall ill because their great-grandfather shed blood or committed some other grave fault (Wilson 1959, 162). Ancestral punishments for the violations of members of the lineage or clan bespeak the condition that the Maori objectify in the "kinship I."

24. Childbirth and warfare are often linked as gendered forms of achieving the same finality, reproduction of the society: childbirth directly; warfare by the appropriation and enculturation of fertile power, as may involve sacrifice and cannibalism. War and childbirth are also widely associated by virtue of the reproductive prowess and marital privileges acquired by successful warriors: as, for example, in Fiji (Clunie 1977) and Amazonia (Fausto 2007). Again, the same relations are ritually combined in marriage by capture (Barnes 1999).

The one entity in discrete subjects is also evident wherever revenge may be taken on any member of the group of a slayer.
Incest among Amazonian Araweté not only spreads the fault
among the offender's kin but also opens their village to an enemy
attack. "Villagers of incestuous people, it is said, used to end up
so riddled with enemies' arrows that vultures were not even able
to peck at the cadavers" (Viveiros de Castro 1992, 163). Exagger-
ated no doubt, but in the Amazon, where enemies are generically
known as potential affines, one can understand why incest would
offend them.[25]

Another manifestation of the co-presence of kinsmen is the
generalization of the injuries suffered by the one to the pain then
endured by the many. The damage may require compensating the
kin of the injured person for the travail thus inflicted on them,
even if the injury was self-inflicted. Kenneth Read relates that a
Gahuku-Gama man (New Guinea Highlands) who cuts his hair
is obliged to recompense his relatives and age-mates. Indeed,
these people go into mourning, "plastering their bodies with clay
and ashes, and perhaps cutting a finger" (Read 1955, 267). The
man who cut his hair must then "make their skin good" by giving
his relatives a pig feast and gifts of valuables. One might think
the punishment did not fit the crime were it not that men typi-
cally cut their hair when going off to European employ or when
they are baptized as Christians, which is to say when they de-
part from the traditional society—as in death.[26] Or again, Sergei
Kan (citing K. Oberg) sees the reason for the analogous conduct

25. Regarding collective responsibility, it seems that a Maori husband may hold his
affines at fault for his wife's breaking wind—or so I read this notice from John White,
transmitted by Johansen: "There was a husband who felt a bad smell under the blanket
of the bed. He thought it was due to his wife and scolded her, i.e., he abused her, her
parents, and her brothers" (1954, 35).

26. Hair-cutting in the New Guinea Highlands apparently has a variety of motivations, although a common theme is the compensation of maternal kin by the patrilineal
clansmen of the child for some loss of maternal life-component in the child, which may
also be relevant in the Gahuku-Gama case (see, e.g., Meggitt 1965; Salisbury 1962, 34).

of Tlingit people in the generalization of suffering to kinsmen, both affinal and consanguineal:

> The face was the main surface upon which the emotions as well as the social identity of the person were depicted. . . . If a man of high status injured his face by falling down, especially in public, he was supposed to remain indoors until the marks had healed, and then give a small feast to his own clan to compensate it for the shame brought to it by his disfigurement. . . . In addition, he and his clan gave a feast to those members of the opposite moiety [i.e., affines] who had witnessed the accident. (Kan 1989, 60–61)

Generally, it is the affines who are importantly compensated in such cases: the spouse-giving people, whose sacrifice (marriage) of one of their members gave life to the injured person; whereas, the home or lineage kin are held collectively responsible and required to pay. On the American Northwest coast, as in Polynesia, an injury or death may evoke ritual attack by the affinal party on the home kin (Kan 1986, 202). The old-time *pakeha* F. W. Maning (1922, 144ff.) relates an incident of this kind among Maori wherein the aggrieved affinal (-*cum*-maternal) kinfolk descended in the guise of a war party on the paternal relatives of a boy who had fallen into a fire and badly burned himself. The injury itself was considered a disgrace, and it was all the worse because the lad was a promising warrior and his family was of some prominence. Led by the boy's mother's brother, the maternal kin made a clean sweep of the paternal property, whatever could be carried off, canoes and all. This was a high compliment to the victims, as Johansen (1954, 141–42) observes, showing that they were persons of some consideration, so that in return the boy's father made a large feast for his affinal robbers.

The converse of the kinship generalization of injuries suffered by an individual is the collective responsibility taken by kinsmen for the well-being of their relative's body. "Each person's body is his kindred," reads an old Irish text (Charles-Edwards 1993, 39). The individual body is a social fact insofar as it is created by the acts and concerns of some community of kinfolk—to which in turn the body owes service in something like a praxis of the "kinship I." Accordingly, morphology is sociology. As "the locus of vested interests of the community," Becker says of Fijian practice, the state of one's body "reflects the achievements of its caretakers. A body is the responsibility of the micro-community that feeds and cares for it; consequently, crafting its form is the province of the community rather than the self" (1995, 59). This can mean that even eating is transpersonal, as Strathern put it more generally for Melanesians:

> Eating . . . is not an intrinsically beneficiary act, as it is taken to be in the Western commodity view that regards the self as thereby perpetuating its own existence . . . rather, in being a proper receptacle for nourishment, the nourished person bears witness to the effectiveness of a relationship with the mother, father, sister's husband or whoever is doing the feeding. . . . Consumption is no simple matter of self-replacement, then, but the recognition and monitoring of relationships. (1988, 294)

Or again, Bamford on Kamea people:

> Bodies do not exist as autonomous entities, but have the capacity to act directly upon one another. Therefore, it is entirely possible for one person to eat for another. . . . So close is the connection between a boy and his mother that the eating habits of one are seen to directly affect the health and well-being of the other. (2007, 6, 62)

It is all like the old line—probably predating the Old Testament—about the Jewish mother who says to her finicky-eater kid, "Eat, eat, or I'll kill myself."

It follows that among kinfolk neither interest nor agency are individual facts—again in contrast to the self-fashioning, self-interested individual as we know him. Perhaps (as in the Tomasello experiments) intention should not be so considered either. It is not simply that one acts for others or on behalf of others, but just as selves are diffused among others, so is agency a function of the conjunction, located in and as the relationship it also realizes in action. Agency is in the unity of the duality; it is an act of we-ness. Alternatively, one could follow Strathern in considering the actor as the agent—the one doing the cooking, cultivating, or fishing, say, for the household—but at the risk of depriving agency of the shared intentionality and causality. For as Strathern notes, "Reciprocal activity within the household comes to symbolize other-directed intentionality. Husband and wife each contribute their work and effort to the household . . ." (1988, 90). And later, of a wife's work: "If the wife is the agent, the one who acts, then her husband is the cause of her acting, though not himself active" (274). So long as "agency" remains a function of the singular person, who is rather functioning in mutual relationships of being, it seems to mean no more than "acting."

On Kinship Solidarities and Conflicts

Broadly speaking, mutuality of being among kinfolk declines in proportion to spatially and/or genealogically reckoned distance. For certain material transactions involving the life-value of persons, such as *wergeld*, the measure of joint being may be more or less precisely determined by the differential compensations awarded to various relatives. The old Irish made calculations of kinship distance for such purposes by reckoning collaterality (among agnatic kin) according to the number of generations from a common ancestor, each degree of which had a different designation (Charles-Edwards 1993; and for an ancient Chinese analogue, Chun 1990). On a similar basis of the life-value of the principal, the exchanges accompanying life-cycle rites in many societies would provide comparable indications of degrees of participatory belonging among the contributors and recipients. But apart from differences in kinship degree, there is a distinction in kind set up by the rules of exogamy between the we-group of "own people" and the "different people" with whom intermarriage is possible.

The "own people," where individuals have their primary affiliation and identity, are characteristically of "one kind," which is the reason for the usual interdiction of marriage between them. Classically constituted as one entity in discrete subjects, the members of the group are united on the basis of a shared participation in ancestry, residence, commensality, land use, or other such media of mutuality. In this regard, they are equal as well as the same, and in principle their relationship is characterized by an unconditional amity. But recall Rupert Stasch on kinship belonging: "The ideal includes its own failure" (2009, 136). Precisely because of the equality, a certain measure of conflict—ranging from studied distance to violent rupture—is possible wherever the primary group holds offices, privileges, or objects of differential value. The lurking contradiction is a discriminatory distribution of social and/or material value among members of a group who are in principle equal and alike. Hence the frequent observations of formality and hostility between brothers and between fathers and sons (in patrilineal orders), by contrast to the ease and warmth of relations with more distant or affinal kin. Rivalry of a similar kind may attend relations between segments of larger kin groups, such as Simon Harrison documents for Manambu people (Sepik region), in this case involving competition for marriageable women:

> This is a competition solely between descent groups. . . . The key material resource in the society is not wealth but reproduction, and the competition for it is between agnates. Subclans of the same exogamous group are, implicitly, permanent rivals for wives and compete for them by offering their marriageables [potential affines] valuable alliance relationships. (1990, 39)

In contrast to the primary exogamous group, the people of one kind, affinal kin are united by a difference. Given the incest tabu, brothers-in-law (and their respective people) are related to one another through a woman who is sister to one and wife to the other, and whose offspring in most instances will have a primary affiliation with one and not the other (Viveiros de Castro 2004,

19).[27] As Nancy Munn describes the dynamics for the Gawa, marriage entails the separation of people who are the same—the brother and sister destined for different connubial fates—and the union of people who are different—the husband and wife who will form a reproductive totality (1986, 41; cf. Huntsman 1981). So if the alliance is centered in the solidarity of marital sexuality, by the same token it is also oppositional, insofar as the kin groups united by intermarriage, in giving or taking spouses, have differentially affected their membership and reproductive potential. Or to put the contradiction otherwise, the exogamous group of kin that autonomously organizes its own existence depends on others for the possibility thereof (LaFontaine 1973, 478). Life comes from outside, from the affines, even as the flow of gifts and respects expressing this external dependence gives persons value and distinction within their own group. In the event, relations of alliance are endemically ambivalent, sometimes notoriously so. The affiliation and services of the out-marrying spouse are usually not so much at issue as his or her reproductive powers, lost to one group in the form of that person's children and gained by another.

This zero-sum game is rarely if ever taken to its conclusion, however, especially insofar as the alliance between kin groups rides on intermarriage. Some degree of conflicting kinship then unites the two parties in the form of the continuing affiliation of one group with certain members of the other, namely, the children born to the other group by their out-marrying member—children upon whom, by their double appurtenance, the intergroup alliance devolves. A significant mutuality of being still joins these children with their maternal relatives in patrilineal orders, with their paternal kin in matrilineal orders, and generally, in most any regime, with the kin of their in-marrying parent. Recall in this connection the offense given to the maternal kin of the Maori boy who fell into the fire and the revenge taken

27. See the discussion of cross-cousins as pure affines in chapter 2.

on the youth's paternal relatives. Another, widely reported aspect of this double bond (*–cum–*double bind) is the so-called "metaphysical influence" of affinal kin, most saliently mother's brothers and father's sisters, endowed with inherent powers of blessing or cursing the relatives of their own who belong to allied groups. Benevolent and malevolent, these intersubjective effects seem appropriate expression of the ambiguities of the alliance and the dual life connections of children, a primary one with the kin of one parent and yet a fateful one with the people of the other parent. It follows that the extent to which the marital metaphysics of mutual being are amicable or conflictual depends on other conditions, including the nature of the descent and marriage systems.

The potential hostility of affinity can be mitigated by prescriptive marriage rules that more or less directly compensate the intermarrying groups for transfers of their reproductive members. On the other hand, complex marital rules—which prohibit unions with a wide variety of kin and thus inhibit repeated alliances between groups—are likely to give rise to the disposition voiced proverbially in the New Guinea Highlands as "we fight the people we marry." The possibility of conflict is one good reason for the customary material exchanges accompanying betrothal and marriage and continuing through the life cycle of the partners, perhaps also the life of their children and beyond. Nyakyusa say, if there is no bride-price, there is no kinship. "A wife for whom cattle have not been given is not my relative. . . . With us relationship is cattle" (Wilson 1950, 121).

For Reite of New Guinea, hostility to affines is axiomatic: men always fight the one with whom their sister has fallen in love and wishes to marry, thus threatening to remove herself from them; it is commonly supposed that she must have been coerced by her lover (Leach 2003, 83). In the view of Wari' people, "brothers-in-law can be seen as enemies with whom one must live rather than make war" (Vilaça 2010, 305). (Perhaps we should adopt the current American teenage jargon "frenemies".

as a technical term.) An important correspondence between a man's relations to brothers-in-law and to beasts of prey is widely reported for Amazonia, inasmuch as both concern the appropriation of external life-sources. Philippe Descola writes of the Achuar: "The behavior of brothers-in-law, based on mutual dependence and indispensable amenities, thus constitutes a model for the ambiguous camaraderie that is an appropriate metaphor for the relationship that binds the hunter to his prey" (1996, 133). In the Amazon (as also in Southeast Asia), we have to do with the reproduction of local society through the predatory exploitation of the life powers of alterity in martial and marital exploits (cf. Sahlins 2008, 2010). Carlos Fausto describes this as a cosmic project of interspecies relations organized by the kinship of affinity:

> In this universe in which nothing is created and everything is appropriated, different groups—human or nonhuman, living or dead—related as meta-affines . . . seek to capture people in order to turn them into relatives. Shamans capture animal spirits and warriors capture enemy spirits, fertilizing women, giving names to children, producing songs for ritual, benefiting the hunt. . . . Predation is thus intimately connected to the cosmic desire to produce kinship. (2007, 502)

Reflecting on the ambivalent relations of marriage, Maori say they want to be like the stars, who effectively live alone and forever. It is similar to the famous ending of Lévi-Strauss's *Elementary Structures of Kinship*, referring to the Sumerian myth of the Golden Age and the Andaman myth of the future life,

> the former placing the end of primitive happiness at a time when the confusion of languages made words into common property, the latter describing the bliss of the hereafter as a heaven where women will no longer be exchanged, i.e., removing to an equally unattainable past or future the joys, eternally denied to social man, of a world in which one might *keep to oneself*. (1969, 497; emphasis in original)

"The Mysterious Effectiveness of Relationality"

In conclusion, a reflection on Eduardo Viveiros de Castro's (2009) golden insight that kinship, gift exchange, and magic are so many different modalities of the same animistic regime. They are so many intersubjective transactions in powers of being, working through the specifically human means of intentionality and influence—thus so many realizations of "the mysterious effectiveness of relationality" (243). This is a world of co-presence, of the relations of specifically *human* being, a world indeed that we have not altogether forsaken.

I judge from Viveiros de Castro's discussion that any one of these—kinship, gift, or magic—may include the others. This is clear enough in a gift economy, "where things and people assume the form of persons" (249; following Gregory 1982, 241). Insofar as the parties reciprocally appropriate things that are inalienably associated with the person of the other, the exchange may create a "fellowship" between them, the intersubjective participation that is the hallmark of kinship. Then again, the intentional deployment of a thing-person in order to produce beneficial effects—a return gift, fellowship—also has the distinctive quality of a magical act.

With regard to the magical register of the animist ontology, Viveiros de Castro invokes Alfred Gell's (1998) argument that magic is not some mistaken version of physical causation, but rather works through purpose and influence: that is, the way people generate effects in one another. One might say, then, that magic is a technique for the transpersonal imposition of being into other subjects—including crops, animals, or anything with subject attributes. By means of commanding, pleading, pleasing, demanding, and so on, magic effects a shared intentionality between the actor and the alter—a corollary of which is their participation in a common regime of personhood. An Achuar offered Philippe Descola a fine example:

Those to whom we sing our *anent* [mute invocations], they do not hear them as you hear me at the moment; they do not hear the words that we speak. But the thoughts that we put into our *anent*, they enter the *wakan* [soul] of those whom we invoke and there they establish themselves, as in a house. Then, without fully realizing it, those for whom we sing desire what we desire. They bend themselves to our thoughts because it is our desires that fill them. (1996, 133)

Note, however, that the intersubjectivity of magic may be coercively introjected, in which respects it is not the same as the mutuality of kinship. Moreover, magic need obey no principle of amity but may indeed be malevolent. Yet by harming or consuming the other, sorcery ("black magic") and witchcraft are quite analogous to failures of kinship, and in such regards they can be included in the same animist ontology, if on the darker side thereof. Indeed, as the consumption or penetration of the body of the other with the intent to harm, witchcraft and sorcery are rather, by definition, negative kinship. "In acting as agents," Edward LiPuma writes of Maring, "sorcerers cannibalize or consume the relations of which they are composed. They literally cannibalize the life force (*min*) of their own kin" (1998, 71).

Then again, failed exchange, insofar as it likewise negates kinship, can have the same deleterious effects on life as sorcery or witchcraft. In Johansen's analyses of pertinent Maori texts, an unrequited gift in one way or another ruptures the fellowship of the parties—that is, their kinship—either by weakening the life of the receiver or draining that of the giver. On one hand, it is said, "the gift is a *mate*, a weakening [or death] to the receiver if he cannot assert himself by counter-gifts." On the other hand, a recipient who fails to give a counter-gift "steals a little of the giver's life instead of making it penetrate into him. The Maori say that he *kaihaus* the gift, which should probably be interpreted to the effect that he consumes (*kai*) the gift as a *hau*, i.e., an object which connects a person with others in a ritual situation, so that he, as it were, drains the giver's life" (1954, 115–16). The apparent contradiction reminds us that gifts may also be poison, or that they make slaves (as Inuit say). Depending on the differences in the quantities, frequencies, and values of the objects exchanged, gifts may well generate inequality, domination, and/or hierarchical inclusion. I gesture here to such politics of kinship practice, but as I am rather concerned with what kinship is, I reserve these issues for other occasions.

Viveiros de Castro sums up his triadic synthesis of kinship, gift exchange, and magic by contrast to a commodity economy, "where things and people assume the form of objects." Where gifts embody subject qualities, however,

> relations between human beings are expressed by classificatory kinship terms—in other words, they are kinship relations. But then, relations between things must be conceived as bonds of magical influence; that is, as kinship relations in object form. The objective world of a 'gift economy' is an animistic ontology of universal agency and trans-specific kinship relatedness, utterly beyond the grasp of the genealogical method—a world where yams are our lineage brothers and roam unseen at night, or where jaguars strip away their animal clothes and reveal themselves as our cannibal brothers-in-law. . . . Indeed, it appears that when these people talk about personification processes, they really mean it. (2009, 243)

Finally, to buckle this (hermeneutic) circle—without, I hope, coming to an undesirable end—it is useful to notice that Viveiros de Castro's exposition of the animistic ontology fundamentally and fruitfully inverts David Schneider's quixotic deconstruction of kinship. Viveiros de Castro and Schneider came to opposite conclusions about the nature and value of kinship from similar understandings of its relations to other dimensions of cultural order. The former's finding of the same animistic regime in the different registers of kinship, gift, and magic in this respect matched the latter's discovery of the *nomos/physis* opposition in kinship, nationalism, and religion. But where Schneider wanted to close down the cultural study of kinship because he concluded from the ontological similarities that it did not exist, Viveiros de Castro's work offers a revelation of a certain cultural order of intersubjectivity in which kinship takes a fundamental place, indeed a cosmic place. Rather than imposing an ancient Western philosophy as an ethnographic epistemology, Viveiros de Castro let the Indians' ontology come to him, their potential brother-in-law, and he made a comparative anthropology of it. Viveiros de Castro's cultural analysis thus goes a long way to explaining how the followers of Schneider's work, by attending to "symbols and meanings," could give new life to the kinship studies he wanted to remove from the anthropological agenda.

2

What Kinship Is Not—Biology

Chapter 1 offered a definition of kinship as "mutuality of being": kinfolk are members of one another, intrinsic to each other's identity and existence. Coming in various degrees and forms, such intersubjective relations of being, I argued, will account for performative or "made" kinship as well as relations of procreation. Persons participate in each other's existence by a variety of meaningful attributes besides the presumed connections of "biology" or even common substance. In New Guinea, as reported by Robert Glasse, "those who behave towards one another in a positive manner regard each other as kin, whether or not they are known or believed to be genealogically related" (1969, 33). As if in confirmation: "A striking pattern here is the frequency with which Korowai describe someone they were not previously related to as having 'become a relative' (*lambi-lelo*) through relations of reciprocal visiting, cooperation, and food-giving" (Stasch 2009, 135). Or then again, consider the Fijian's response to the naïve question of the ethnographer:

"Suppose two men, one a relative of yours and one not, had something you needed, which would you go to [to *kerekere*, 'request aid']"? The reply was to this effect: "I would go to my relative of course. If he didn't give it to me, and the other man did, I would know that the other man was really my relative." (Sahlins 1962, 204)

Although ethnography testifies that these peoples and numerous others expressly accord kinship status to persons with whom they have no genealogical connection, many anthropologists, not to mention sociobiologists and evolutionary psychologists, have long contended that the relationships in question are only "metaphors" of kinship, or else they are "fictive kinship," precisely because no biogenetic relationship is involved. "Real kinship" is the relationships established by birth—as we might know from our own concepts of "blood" kin. As Harold Scheffler and Floyd Lounsbury wrote in a well-known monograph: "Relations of genealogical connection" are "kinship proper"; moreover, they are "fundamentally different from and are logically and temporally prior to any social relations of kinship" (1971, 38)—which would apparently rule out any performative constitution of kinship *a priori*. (In any case, this can't possibly be so, for sexual intercourse is not prior to the social relations between persons, rules of marriage, etc.). Again, as Scheffler put it, persons related by birth are relatives "by definition" (1976, 76). Birth relations comprise the "distinctive feature" of what he calls "the central, primary, or principal category of 'relatives'": a person is "ego's relative if and only if he or she is the genitor or genitrix, or offspring, or related to ego through some chain of relationships of this kind."[1] Going back another few decades, the argument was very much the same, as in the text from the *American Anthropologist* of 1937 penned by the eminences Kingsley Davis and W. Lloyd Warner:

---

1. Scheffler has made many admirable analyses of kinship on the basis of birth relationships, but he explicitly (and unusually) refuses to call them "biological," because what is at issue are the people's various concepts of procreation and the connections thus generated (see Scheffler and Lounsbury 1971, 37ff.).

... kinship may be defined as social relationships based on connection through birth. This holds for relationships by affinity as well as for those by consanguinity—for although husband and wife may have no recognized common ancestry, they are nonetheless related by blood through their common offspring. Even relatives by adoption are relatives only in so far as they are treated *as if* they belong to the family by reproduction. Whenever one finds two relatives, no matter which two, there are one or more births (real or fictitious) connecting them. It makes no difference what conception of reproduction the particular culture may have. (1937, 292; emphasis in original)

The determination of kinship relations as genealogical connections has been dominant in the anthropology of kinship ever since Lewis Henry Morgan founded the subject on that premise in *Systems of Consanguinity and Affinity in the Human Family* (1871). Few concessions have been made to later ethnographic reports, none on the essential matter of the biological basis. One, however, is that the biological basis is "folk biology." The relations of procreation and birth turn out to be culturally relative, differently understood in different societies according to the local "theory of reproduction." This so-called "theory" usually remains unexamined, however, on the supposition, as Davis and Warner had it, that "it makes no difference." Secondly, the network of actual genealogical relations is variously inflected by other social considerations, particularly by different descent schemes. This again makes no difference—if it is not an analytical virtue, allowing us to know systems of descent with some precision. Thus Ernest Gellner, for instance, contends:

Kinship structure *means* the manner in which a pattern of physical relationships is made use of for social purposes, . . . the way in which a physical criterion is used for the selection of members for a group and the ascription of rights, duties, etc. . . . But the elements of the physical pattern are essentially simple and universal, whilst the social patterns imposed on it are highly diversified and complex.

And it is just this, the existence of the universal and simple physical substrate, which makes it possible to describe descent systems with some precision and compare them meaningfully. (1960, 193; emphasis in original)

And finally, the immediate relations of birth—the genitor and genetrix of a given Ego and their other offspring, as Scheffler has it—are "primary," both in the sense that they are the focal instances of kin categories and that terms used for them are extended to other relatives, or are derived from them by reducing the specificity of the attributes by which primary kin are defined. The further extension of kinship terms proper to persons assumed or known to be without genealogical connection may be analytically allowed as "kinship" on an "as if" basis; or disallowed as metaphorical; or else, in the usual academic mode of "the answer lies somewhere in-between," taken to indicate that the kinship order is a combination of biologically given and culturally constructed relationships.

This chapter is an argument against all such "biological" understandings of kinship: not only because they are encompassed in meaningful determinations of "mutuality of being"; or because postnatal, "made" kinship often enough takes priority over relations of procreation; or because the latter are culturally variable, sometimes to the point that they are of no particular interest to the people concerned; but also importantly because the relations of birth are reflexes of the greater kinship order and are incorporated within that order. If, in regard to the last, children are conceived, say, from the "blood" of the mother and the "sperm" of the father, these are not mere physiological substances of reproduction but meaningful social endowments of ancestral and affinal identities and potencies. For they link the child to others with whom the parents are known to share such substances. It follows that what is reproduced in the birth is a system of kinship relations and categories in which the child is given a specific position and positional value. It likewise follows that kinship is a thoroughly symbolic-*cum*-cultural phenomenon—as Lévi-Strauss said, for all his lingering nostalgia for the "biological family":

> Of course, the biological family is ubiquitous in human society. But what confers upon kinship its socio-cultural character is not what it retains from nature, but, rather, the essential way in which it diverges from nature. A kinship system does not consist in the objective ties of descent or consanguinity between individuals. It exists only in human consciousness; it is an arbitrary system of representations, not the spontaneous development of a real situation. . . . The essence of human kinship is to require the establishment of relations among what Radcliffe-Brown calls "elementary families." Thus, it is not the families (isolated terms) that are truly "elementary," but, rather, the relations between those terms. (1964, 50–51)

Contrary, however, to an anthropology of kinship whose elementary forms are relationships, the long-standing determinations of kinship from the position of an Ego and his or her "primary" kin suggest that a consistent complement of the going biologism in kinship studies is an equally entrenched egocentrism. Even before Malinowski foolishly claimed he was present at the origin of classificatory kinship when he saw a Trobriand child apply the term he had learned for "father" to his father's brother, kinship has too often been analyzed from the way it is lived and learned by individuals, as if a domestic logic of cognition were the *raison d'être* of the system. The kinship organization of the society is conflated with the way it is acquired by an (abstract) individual in the context of his or her nuclear family. Indeed, the way it is acquired is taken for how it came to be. Hence the supposed "primacy" of "elementary" family relations, the sense that people may have that these are the "true brothers," "true mothers," etc., and that such familial terms are extended outward through genealogical connections to form kinship classes. A socially constituted network of relationships between persons and among groups is thus dissolved into the logic of its cognition by an individual subject (as in componential analysis).

Society is subsumed in and as the individual's experience of it. Welcome to America . . .

Kinship Is Thicker than Blood

We already know (from chapter 1) that in many societies the genealogical relations of reproduction are in diverse ways matched—if they are not completely ignored—as sources of kinship by postnatal considerations of mutuality of being. Here I offer further examples specifically concerned with the subordination of birth relations to performative and pragmatic kinship. In this connection, it will be worthwhile first to revisit the reproductive complex of the Ku Waru (Nebilyer Valley, New Guinea).

As documented by Francesca Merlan and Alan Rumsey, for Ku Waru people the reproductive transmission of substance has no privilege over substantive connections established by social action, inasmuch as the source of both is the same: the soil, whence comes the "grease" (*kopong*) that is "the essential matter of living organisms, both animal and vegetable" (1991, 42). Such grease enters into the conception of the child through the father's sperm and mother's milk, both of which are also called *kopong*. But as *kopong* is also present in sweet potatoes and pork, the same kind of substantial connection to other persons can be achieved nutritively, as by sharing food or eating from the same land. In this way, children or grandchildren of immigrants may be fully integrated with local people as kinsmen; and for that matter, the offspring of two brothers are as much related because they were sustained by the same soil as because their fathers were born of the same parents. Merlan and Rumsey comment:

> In Western ideologies 'real' siblingship is determined entirely by prenatal influences: by the fact that the corporeal existence of each sibling began with an event of conception at which genetic substance was contributed by the same two individuals. . . . Ku Waru discourse about reproduction appears not to entail any such notion of genetic substance. Rather, *kopong* figures at every stage in the reproductive

process as a kind of *nutritive* substance, whether extracted directly
from the gardens, channeled through a man's reproductive organs,
woman's breast, or stored and consumed in the flesh of a pig. In contrast to the western one, there is in this view no essential difference
between pre-natal and post-natal influences in their power to make
us what we are. (43; emphasis in original)

Birth here is not simply a human genetic process, and insofar
as the soil that is the source of kinship connections is clan land,
the "extension" of kin terms beyond so-called primary relatives
is always already built into the relations of reproduction. The
schematics of human births reference the kinship matrix of the
individual they compose. Here, then, is another modality of a
fundamental argument of this chapter, to which I will repeatedly return: that kinship is the *a priori* of birth rather than the
sequitur. Referencing the kinship matrix of the individual they
compose, the relations of reproduction issue in children whose
destiny as social beings was present from the creation.

Besides the common means of establishing kinship in life
rather than in utero—such as co-residence, commensality, living
off the same land, friendship, etc.—such practices of participation in one another's existence are indefinitely many, inasmuch
as they are culturally relative. One may be kin to another by being born on the same day (Inuit), by following the same tabus
(Araweté), by surviving a trial at sea (Truk) or on the ice (Inuit),
even by mutually suffering from ringworm (Kaluli). Somewhat
more widely distributed is kinship through name-sharing between living persons, whereby the name-receiver takes on the
personage and relationships of the name-giver, whether or not
they were kin before. Not to be confused with the common Inuit practices of naming a child after a deceased relative, name-
sharing with the living is known to Belcher Island Inuit (Guemple 1965), !Kung Bushmen (Marshall 1957), Ojibway (Landes
1969), and a number of Gê-speaking peoples of central Brazil
(Seeger 1981; Da Matta 1982; Lave, Stepick, and Sailer 1977; Melatti 1979; among others). This homonymous kinship is worth
some discussion here, at once for notions of shared being that

are completely independent of bodily connections and that are much more prevalent than relations of birth. In the exceptional case that proves this rule, kinship is virtually exclusively based on name-sharing.

So far as shared being is concerned, the intersubjectivity is total: namesakes are a single person; the name-receiver takes on the identity of the name-giver. So Ruth Landes reported for Ojibway:

> Ego and the namer of ego are "namesakes" and by definition one and the same person. . . . [By] naming I have given someone a portion of that power which is I. . . . The namesake term seems analyzable as "my body" or "my self." (1969, 23, 117, 117n)

Likewise, Anthony Seeger for Suya of Central Brazil:

> The male name-receiver is said to be the exact replica of his name-giver in ceremonial affairs. . . . The Suya maintain there is an actual identity between the two, that in some sense they are one being. (1981, 141)

Or !Kung Bushmen, according to Lorna Marshall:

> The !Kung believe that the name is somehow part of the entity of a person and that when one is named for a person one partakes of that person's entity in some degree. . . . The !Kung have put to good use the belief that persons who have the same name partake of each other's entities. (1957, 22–23; see also Lave, Stepick, and Sailer 1977; Guemple 1965, 328)

Name-sharing relationships are thus reminiscent of Aristotle's determination of kinship as "the same entity in discrete subjects." Name-sharers call each other reciprocally by the same term, such as the Inuit "bone" (*saunik*) or Ojibway "my body" (*niiawaa*). Like other kin, they respect particular rules of conduct toward each other, usually including responsibilities that can be described as life-giving, such as providing material aid when needed or taking an important role in a name-receiver's life-crisis rites. It is reported for Belcher Islanders that names embody and thus transmit to name-receivers the status, character, or attributes of the name-giver (Guemple 1965, 328)—an observation that in many other societies could pass for what parents transmit to children by birth. And among the other aspects of their kinship, there exists between name-giver and name-receiver that "mysterious effectiveness of relationality" by which what one does or suffers happens to the other (see chapter 1). Guemple invokes Leach's notion of "mystical influence [of affines]" in this connection, such that between namesakes "feelings of anger and resentment, and socially reprehensible conduct, are reciprocally detrimental, especially in matters of hunting efficacy and health" (329). Harboring ill thoughts, one may thus endanger the life of one's name-sharer.

Being the one person, a name-receiver takes on the name-giver's kinship relations and addresses them accordingly; and they use the appropriate terms in return. This may hold even if the name-sharers are of opposite sexes, as is possible for Ojibway, so that the parents of a female name-giver will then call her male namesake "daughter." Often the namer and namesake were otherwise related before sharing the former's name rearranged their kinship. On the other hand, people who had no previous relationship may enter into homonymous kinship. Or else, upon first meeting, strangers may determine their kinship transitively if either has the same name as some kin of the other (Bushmen). In Guemple's study of the Belcher *saunik*, or "bone," system, he found:

> All of the terms of the *saunik* system take precedence over other forms of address and reference, including names, nicknames, diminutive names and genealogically-derived kinship terms. . . . In the most general case, any Ego can address and refer to the relatives of anyone whose name is the same as his (i.e., namesake, namegiver, or namesharer) by the appropriate terms used by that other in addressing and referring to them. . . . He may also address and refer to anyone having the same name as any of his kinsmen . . . by the

term he applies to that kinsman. . . . Ideally, there is no limitation in the range of persons to whom Ego can relate using skewed [i.e., non-genealogically derived] terms, and it sometimes happens that he will exploit name identity to relate to persons to whom no known (or imaginable) genealogical connection can be traced. (1965, 326, 330–31)

Belcher Islanders are perhaps unique in applying relationships derived from name-sharing to "primary" kin. Gê-speaking peoples and others maintain their nuclear family relationships. For Belcher Inuit, however, it appears that homonymous kinship is even more solidary: "Persons who reside together, either in a single household or a camp, or who are regularly involved in joint effort of some kind (hunting, fishing, etc.), even if these are members of Ego's nuclear family, are commonly identified by skewed terms in address and/or reference" (331).

Belcher Inuit are not unique, however, in thus overriding genealogical relations for homonymous kinship when they have the option. Most name-sharing peoples prefer name-derived relationships over "genealogical" ones outside the household. As, for example, the Suya, of whom it is reported: "Naming terminology always overrides all other kinship, as does ceremonial kinship terminology" (Seeger 1981, 142; see Lave, Stepick, and Sailer 1977; Marshall 1957, 7). And everywhere, the effect is a community of kinfolk related largely or primarily through naming relations—the "skewed" terms of the Inuit—rather than those that follow from procreation and filiation. Virtually the whole community may be ordered by kin relationships that are arbitrary from the point of view of genealogical connections. The Krahó, for example: "A given Krahó normally calls all other Krahó, with the exception of his closest relatives, by the relationship terms which are applied to those people by the individuals who bestowed names on the speaker" (Melatti 1979, 59). Indeed, name-sharing may be the fundamental means of extending kinship widely beyond the residential community. Using name relationships, the !Kung Bushmen of Nyae-Nyae are able to spread kinship in all directions, as much as one hundred miles away. "The !Kung who live in this region are not *ia dole* [strangers] to each other. The name-relationships make them feel they are one people" (Marshall 1957, 24).

It can hardly be claimed that name kinship is a metaphor, given that it has the essential qualities of kin relationships everywhere—notably the attributes of intersubjective participation—whether or not the parties are genealogically connected. But for all that, a problem remains: viz., that all these postnatal determinations of kinship, including those for which no genealogical connection can be imagined, are nevertheless formulated in (apparently) genealogical terms. New Guinean men who are nourished from the same soil, being common offspring of the land, are thereby "brothers" to one another. The name kinship of !Kung Bushmen is not different from the ostensibly genealogical determination of relationship terms; it is only that the parties involved adopt each other's kinship statuses. Does it not follow, then, that the relations derived from procreation comprise the primary "code" or "model" of all human kinship? Or that such "true" relations of genealogy provide the "focus" or "type species" of kinship categories? Moreover, are not these "primary" terms the means by which anthropologists analytically determine a domain of kinship in various societies? Never mind the irony that the biological premise has to be saved by a kind of "fictive kinship," in the end is not kinship founded on biological relationships?

The Kinship Mode of Human Reproduction

If I read him correctly, Robert McKinley (1981, 2001), in innovative discussions of the problem, while acknowledging that kinship terminology has a genealogical component, denies the implication that the genealogical-*cum*-biological meanings are "primary." They comprise rather a "folk biology" that itself expresses the larger principles of kinship order, including (one presumes) the relations of marriage, filiation, and descent. As he puts it: "A more appropriate understanding of the situation is that *the entire terminological system speaks in a genealogical idiom about the relations among social positions"* (1981, 359; emphasis in original). In this connection comes an explanatory footnote:

> I now examine the terminological system. In doing this it will be necessary to refer indirectly to what seems to be the biological system *but only as this has been culturally appropriated by the system of terminology.* . . . Here it is important to recognize that genealogical reckoning is already a way of placing a cultural construction on supposedly preexisting biological facts. But even more important is for us to recognize that what seems to be an element of biological or genealogical information in the referential meaning of kinship vocabulary is, in fact, the use of a metaphor borrowed from folk biology to express the relational properties of the social positions which compose a kinship system. Kinship is a way of being socially connected and folk biology provides the closest conceptual model for this type of linkability. (1981, 386; emphasis in original)

Following McKinley, one might well reverse the received wisdom on the primacy of birth relations, for insofar as these are secondary formations, derivative of the schemes of social order, birth is the metaphor.

Indeed, primary terms are already metaphorical from a biological standpoint, insofar as local modes of reproduction may deny any substantive connection between one or another parent—or even both parents—and their children. We have seen examples in chapter 1, including reproduction by reincarnation, and more will follow. Or consider the !Kung Bushmen, just discussed: given their general organization on a non-genealogical (name-sharing) basis, one can understand why !Kung people—although they believe that the father's semen unites with the mother's blood to form a child—do not invoke such connections in referring to close kin but speak of them simply as their "own people" (Marshall 1957, 13). It follows that the most general acceptation of parent-child and sibling terms is not biological but sociological: they describe domestic and familial relations of coexistence, the full mutuality of being in quotidian social practice, whence their appropriateness to performative and classificatory relations of the same intersubjective quality.

Still, the decisive fallacy in the argument that biological relations constitute "primary" kinship, which is then extended to others by secondary considerations, is that it takes the parents of the child out of their social contexts and presumes they are abstract beings, without any identity except a genital one, who produce an equally abstract child out of the union of their bodily substances. Here is a whole complex of generic humans: an ego, his or her genitor, genetrix, and their offspring, all without social identity, linked through the equally undetermined relations of birth. In the long anthropological tradition that birth relations *as locally conceived* comprise the biogenetic bases of kinship, rarely if ever have scholars who so argue attempted to account for these culturally specific notions of procreation. It is as if these were just so many mistaken ideas of the physiology of conception. All around the world, people got the facts of life wrong, but that's what they have been talking about—a presumption that preserves the appearances of the abstract model. Hence, the question of what motivates these diverse concepts of human reproduction remains unasked and unanswered. What if the mother's blood were the blood of her own mother (and brother, etc.) or of her lineage, and what if the father's semen came from the soil of the clan? Unlike the Robinsonades of the economists, we are not dealing with a lone man and woman copulating on a desert island and thus producing a society. As parents, they already have kinship identities and relationships, the specific logics and attributes of which are transmitted even in the substances they convey to their offspring. For where they are relevant, the blood, milk, semen, bone, flesh, spirit, or whatever of procreation are not simply physiological phenomena, nor do they belong to the parents alone. They are, as I have said, meaningful social endowments that situate the child in a broadly extended and specifically structured field of kin relationships. Through such substances, the child is *ipso facto* connected to wider circles of paternal and maternal relatives—let alone all those implicated when conception also involves bestowals from ancestral beings. So again, "biological" relations being social relations, in such cases the nexus of so-called extended kinship is already in the composition of the fetus.

Consider the implications if the "blood" a mother contributes to the fetus is indeed the blood of her mother. What wider relationships might thus be logically entailed and sociologically inscribed in the relations of procreation? For one, it follows that the child will be related from birth to her mother's sister in the same way she is related to the woman who bore her—her mother and her mother's sister having the same blood (from their mother). And the child will then be related to her mother's sister's children in the same way she is related to her "own" brother and sister, all having this maternal blood. As I say, we are not dealing with a couple reproducing all alone on a desert island. Yet not only is classificatory kinship thus built into procreation, but such conceptual transmissions help explain how and why in so many societies parallel cousins (children of one's mother's sister and father's brother) are distinguished from cross-cousins (children of one's mother's brother and father's sister). This has been a long-standing issue of debate in kinship studies, and not easily resolved, because the special forms of marriage and descent that might account for this opposition of parallel and cross-relatives are not as widely distributed as the phenomenon. However, a distinction between maternal and paternal contributions to the fetus—such as blood and semen or flesh and bone—would be structurally sufficient (Busby 1997); and at the same time, it would be consistent with affinal relationships in a wide array of kinship systems, with or without descent groups of whatever dispensation—matrilineal, patrilineal, bilineal, ambilateral, etc. (cf. Sheffler and Lounsbury 1971; Hornborg 1988).[2] For where the paternal and maternal substances of conception are different in kind and significant in practice, the child will share a certain

2. At some level—e.g., sexual "fluids"—the parental contributions may be generically the same while still being otherwise different in quality or of distinct strains.

parental being through procreation with all parallel cousins and none in this way with cross-cousins. Given the incest tabu, the child has the same maternal blood as her mother's sister's children, but not her mother's brother's children, since they have a different maternal source; and the same paternal substance as her father's brother's children, but not her father's sister's children, since they have a different paternal source. Thus, cross-cousins would not be the "consanguineal" relatives they appear to be in our misleading kinship diagrams and genealogical notions (Dumont, 1953, 1963). More precisely, they would not be consubstantial kin, and accordingly they may well be good to marry. In a fine analysis of just such differential transmissions of substance by gender in Dravidian kinship systems of India, Cecilia Busby writes: "The cross cousins have mothers who are unrelated to each other, and fathers who are unrelated to each other. Hence they are themselves as little related to each other as they could be: they are in fact potential spouses" (1997, 38).[3]

In any case, it is high time to investigate these culturally variable conceptions of conception, and although I can hardly claim to do the subject justice, I offer here a few brief notices of what is ethnographically at stake. Again, at stake is the hypothesis that relations of procreation are patterned by the kinship order in which they are embedded: accordingly, they will vary in the matter of which parent contributes what, if anything, to the composition of the child; and, likewise, what spiritual, behavioral, or morphological characteristics are bestowed by relevant third parties. Inasmuch as genealogical connections entail such

3. Again, the present argument supposes that affinity is structurally salient and functionally significant, hence the relevance of maternal and paternal substances. (Cross-cousins, incidentally, would be affines in the same way as brothers-in-law and other "in-laws" inasmuch as they are differentially connected through a common third party, the paternal relative of one being the maternal relative of the other.) Note that the same substance relations that assimilate siblings and parallel cousins may also be used to differentiate them, insofar as the former share both parental substances and the latter only one. Of course, I am not arguing that kin relations are necessarily tied thus to births, let alone substances, as much of *What Kinship Is—And Is Not* will show.

attributes, they are not logically or temporally prior to culture, let alone to kinship. Indeed, inasmuch as gender and fertility are at issue, there is a good logical chance that relations of human reproduction involve attributes of cosmic dimensions, that they represent human modes of universal powers and processes of fertility.

One caveat, however: these are not so many "theories of conception," as anthropologists are wont to say. For the peoples concerned, they are not *theories* but the known facts of life. Moreover, they are socially significant facts, not just organic processes. It is probably better not to speak of "biology" at all, folk or otherwise, since few or no peoples other than Euro-Americans understand themselves to be constructed upon—or in fundamental ways, against—some biological-corporeal substratum. For many, their kinship is already given in their flesh—as in the following ethnographic reports:

In the hierarchical structures of mother's brother's daughter (MBD) marriage (generalized exchange) of eastern Indonesia, where wife-givers generally outrank wife-takers, the transmission of mother's "blood" is the salient feature of procreation—inasmuch as it is also the reproduction of power and wealth. The emphasis on the "flow of life" through maternal blood may be accompanied by a relative neglect of the father's contribution, notably his "blood," as well as some devaluation of, if not disinterest in, any other substantive aspect of reproduction (Fox 1980). Susan McKinnon (1991, 110) relates that the people of the Tanimbar Islands, although not particularly prudish, are reluctant to talk about sexual fluids or the process of human reproduction—except when it comes to "mother's blood." This alone is the bodily substance that is freely, "in fact, obsessively," talked about. Although it appears that fathers are also linked to their offspring by "blood," the Tanimbarese "continually stress that the ultimate origin of blood is the side of the mother." Note that in a system of MBD marriage and patrilineal descent, the father's maternal blood is the same as the mother's, inasmuch as the father's mother comes from the same group as his wife, ego's mother. And such maternal blood, as McKinnon observes, is not only associated with life; it underlies the idea of kin relationship and defines "the universe of kin"—a bit more than birthing a child:

> In the midst of what is otherwise a striking vagueness on the subject of bodily substances, one thing stands out with marked clarity: blood is a vital substance that is intimately associated with life, and its flow defines both the universe of kin and the commonality that underlies the idea of relation. (1991, 110)

Without going into the rich detail of McKinnon's account, it only needs be added here that the procreative role of the father is undeveloped relative to mother's blood not only because of redundancy but because the greater political system of the Tanimbarese, as well as the main circulation of wealth, is ordered by the asymmetric relations of wife-takers to wife-givers, and the dues the former owe the latter as the source of their life (mother's blood). Paternal descent is the given or unmarked condition compared to the politics of maternal blood. As F. A. E. van Wouden famously observed of eastern Indonesia, asymmetric MBD marriage "is the pivot on which turns the activity of social groups"— even as their human society is thus organized in the same way as the cosmos (1968, 2). Just so, in the analogous case of the Mambai of Timor, Elizabeth Traube notes that, conceived as a line of men, the house is "both immutable and stable"; whereas the ties a house contracts through women are "both mutable and fertile." Hence, "social life is based on a complementary balance between a stable male order and a dynamic female order" (1986, 96).

The Makassae of Timor, as reported by Shepard Forman (1980, 159ff.), offer an exemplary instance of the cosmology of human reproduction. Like the Tanimbarese, they practice MBD marriage, wife-givers being superior to wife-takers, although in procreation each contributes essentially similar child-making substances. Father and mother "join together the force of our veins," the "white blood" (semen) and the red blood that form the child. Moreover, the associated exchanges of bride-wealth and food between the paternal and maternal kin mediate a certain connection between human birth and cosmic fertility. Comprised of work animals, gold, cloth, and other valuables, the wealth passing from wife-takers to wife-givers is reciprocated by cooked rice and pork—which are the source of the bloods that make a child. The exchange, observes Forman, "is a statement about the extension of life through agricultural production and sexual reproduction" (160). Food is the flesh of Mother Earth or her children, and it grows by the complementary action of the dew, which is Father Sky's sperm, and the rain, which is his blood. Forman explains:

> According to the Makassae, dew . . . enters plants through their leaves and mingles with the moisture [blood?] produced by the decay of our dead bodies, which when buried return to Mother Earth's womb, thereby giving life to root crops, maize, rice, and coconuts and filling their fruits with liquid and making them grow. Blood flows in rivulets, . . . the veins of Mother Earth, to the sea. There, male and female bloods unite and rise to the clouds, before returning to earth as life-giving rain. (161)

Forman goes on to document how, in the further affinal roles in mortuary exchanges and the rebuilding of sacred houses, the lineage, too, is fashioned from the same life components. At birth the child is already akin to members of his lineage and the forces of the universe. No "extension" of kinship is needed.

For an informative contrast, by virtue of the distinct and complementary endowments of paternal and maternal elements to the child, consider the procreative complex of the matrilineal Tlingit of the American Northwest Coast. Again, the mode of reproduction represents in its own terms a larger system of relations between groups, as mediated by the rules of marriage (Kan 1986, 1989). Every Tlingit village is composed of the members of exogamous matri-moieties, which are in turn divided into exogamous clans and lineages or houses. The commonly preferred marriage of men to their patrilateral cross-cousins (FZD), when strictly followed, has the effect of reciprocal exchange of husbands between matrilineal groups in successive generations: the son of a man who has gone to reproduce another house returns to do the same for his father's natal group. Even where the lesser segments of the moiety do not practice a strict reciprocity, marriage with a classificatory FZD produces the same exchange of men at the level of the moieties.[4] Although the moieties are co-present in Tlingit villages, each is considered an "outside tribe" or "stranger" to the other. Here is an inner-and-own/outer-and-other relationship between intermarrying groups, a relationship that is reproduced in the smallest microcosm of procreation and the universal system of cosmic powers—thereby instantiating the one in the other.

The inner core of the Tlingit child, consisting of bones and spiritual attributes possessed by the matrilineal ancestors, is the legacy of the mother. The matrikin apparently contribute as well to the outside, the body and flesh that house and protect that inner core of true self, but the face of the child in particular, as well as important behavioral characteristics, come from the father. Yet note the presence of a third, spiritual party in procreation, the maternal ancestors. The effect is not only to counterpose a maternal inside to a paternal outside, but a generic and collective inner self to the external and individualizing component of the face and personality attributes provided by the father, the affinal "stranger" from the opposed moiety. Interesting that this set of contrasts replicate in procreation the relations between the allied houses of the parents in ritual, economic, and political practice.

Outsiders, the father's people support the life and shape the destiny of their child of the other moiety. Taking central roles in the child's life-crisis rites, they thus transform him or her into reproductive adults and persons of value. For children of rank, this includes the paternal ministrations that launch a chiefly career. The father and his people sponsor ceremonies and partici-

---

4. More problematically, it is said that chiefs may practice MBD marriage, which might well produce an asymmetrical (ranked) effect in the marital relations between houses, although still a reciprocal relation of spouse exchange between moieties.

pate in potlatches that endow his son (of the opposite moiety) with the bodily attributes and status of aristocracy. Analogously, the paternal kin are responsible for carving the crests that distinguish their affines' houses. They give face to the house as they do to the child. The crests represent the animal spirits that are the sources of the maternal kin's well-being. This ability to transform the powers of the wild into fundamental domestic spirits of their affines is the corollary of the outside status of the paternal kin—for indeed it is the forces outside and greater than society that bestow its fertility and prosperity. For their services of empowerment, the father's people are in turn gifted and feasted by their affines.

The same relations between internal-maternal and external-paternal obtain among the matrilineal Tsimshian—as Margaret Seguin Anderson describes:

> Tsimshian saw symbolic associations between fathers, foreigners, animals and supernaturals. A father contributed food to his wife and children, members of a *waap* [house, local lineage] different from his own, as animals fed their bodies to humans who lived in a world other than their own. Just as the real animal remained in its own village, the reality of the father remained part of his own *waap*. Members of father's clan had special ritual duties to a child, and were paid by the matriclan for these duties at feasts. (2004, 419)

But return for a moment to the collective ancestral identity bestowed by the Tlingit mother in conception practice, likewise in contrast to the individualizing contribution of paternal substance. Here, in the transmission of a collective matrilineal nature is an evident contradiction of the supposed "primacy" of the kinship of procreation, which is then allegedly extended to distant classificatory kin. Again, it is rather the other way around. The larger relations of ancestry and descent, which is also to say the siblingship of the matrilineal clan as well as affinal connections, are here introjected into the relations of procreation. In such respects, the child is at birth an instance of classificatory categories as well as a specific kin-person in a network thereof.

Nancy Munn describes a very similar mode of matrilineal reproduction among Gawa Islanders of the Melanesian Massim. For Gawa likewise, facial appearance is the paternal (affinal) contribution to the child: a contingent and external contribution, as Munn observes, involving "the domain of relationality to the other, or to an extrinsic, external order"; whereas the blood coming from the mother binds the fetus substantially and enduringly to "the other who is the interior self," the matrikin and the ancestors (1986, 143).[5] On the other hand, a very clear example of the like in a patrilineal order appears in Mervyn Meggitt's classic work (1965) on the lineage system of the Mae-Enga (New Guinea Highlands).

For the Enga, the integration of the ancestral group in the composition of the fetus is already implied by the local definition of the clan as "a line of men begotten by the one penis" (Meggitt 1965, 8). In effect, then, all members of the clan have the same father: they are generically siblings, at least those of the same generation. But it is especially the practices of complex marriage (in the Lévi-Straussian sense) that help explain the encompassment of the system of patrilineal groups, own and affinal, within the relations of procreation. The distinctive feature of complex marriage rules is that they specify categories of persons, mainly relatives, one cannot marry, such that the positive determination of whom one may marry becomes the default case of anyone not prohibited. Thus negatively phrased, the Enga marriage proscriptions are many and extensive. Besides women from one's own clan, the rules stipulate that a man should not marry any female descendant of any living or dead woman of one's own clan; any woman of the subclans of the husbands of women of one's own clan; any woman of the subclans of one's father's mother, mother's mother, and mother's father; any woman of the subclans of wives of living men of one's own patrilineage; and more.

5. This inner being of the matrikin vs. facial endowment of the affinal, father's kin is also found in the Trobriands. It seems to be a widespread systematic aspect of matrilineal descent regimes.

Enga explain that they want to extend their affinal relationships as widely as possible, hence without duplication, and in this way achieve optimal returns for their bride-wealth payments in political and economic alliances. But this is only possible because of the collective way the proscriptions are phrased in terms of lineages, subclans, and clans. A marriage thus implicates whole patrilineal groups as such in affinal relationships, albeit in the non-repetitive way of a single union. Moreover, inasmuch as any given patrilineal group holds the different marriages of its individual members in common, the matrilateral ties will not differentiate the generic "sibling" identities of lineage or clanmates. Rather, "the stress on agnation as an organizing principle is so marked that marriage ties in themselves do little to differentiate individuals or sibling groups within the patrilineage or clan" (Meggitt 1965, 158). Although the relationships of mother's brother and their maternal nephews are especially solidary, the life-giving ministrations of children by their matrilateral kin are apparently limited—as is also consistent with the customary integration of wives in their husband's agnatic groups. Indeed, the Enga famously fight the same people they marry, taking wives in one-off unions with nearby clans with whom they may well be in competition. Probably the several ambivalences of affinity are in play in the equally famously antithetical relationships of Enga men and women, especially in matters of sexuality, and their respective contributions to the makeup of children.

For present purposes, what is significant about the makeup of Enga children is the relative devaluation of the father's substantive contribution to the fetus in favor of the spiritual bestowals of the patrilineal clan ancestor—which is also to say that the so-called primary kinship of fatherhood is secondary to the extended brotherhood of the clan. A child is conceived by the mingling of paternal semen and menstrual blood in the mother's womb. However, four months after conception, "a spirit animates the foetus and gives it an individual personality." Coming from the paternal side, this spirit is not, however, transmitted through the father's semen. As Meggitt tells:

Instead it [the spirit] is in some way implanted by the totality of ancestral ghosts of the father's clan and seems to be an emanation of their generalized potency. . . . The existence of the ancestral ghosts is thus as necessary for the birth of a normal child as the initial conjunction of semen and menstrual blood. (163)

Moreover, in "people's everyday comments on human conception and childbirth,"

they place little emphasis on the father's biological role and are more concerned with the acquisition of a spirit and ultimately of a social identity as a consequence of the father's clan membership. The father's agnatic affiliation legitimately relates the child both by descent and through ritual to a group of clan ancestral ghosts. (163)

People also stress that the mother's blood, producing the child's skin and flesh, provides the outward bodily components that enclose and in effect protect the inward spiritual elements of the clan—although, as noted, the former do not create the child's individuality. But just as singular affinal relationships engage the patrilineal totalities of lineages, subclans, and clans, so the collective identities of the marriage are then realized in the constitution of the one child. Once again, the "extended" kinship category is already present in the so-called primary relationships. The larger structures and values of society are realized in the microcosm of human reproduction.

Very similar collective determinations of kinship in the relations of procreation can be found in African societies that are likewise organized in corporate patrilineal or matrilineal groups, as Karla Poewe (1981) has recognized. Respectively emphasizing the paternal or maternal role in conception, the procreation concepts of the patrilineal Zulu or the matrilineal Luapula people, for example, "somehow show how kin are equated." The Zulu *isithunzi*, the clan ancestral shades, are "present in the procreative act," concentrated in the paternal semen, which "contributes the fundamental makeup of the male or female foetus" (8). Emerg-

ing from the earth, the ancestral shades endow the child with
clan characteristics, to return to the earth at the latter's death.
The clan ancestors of the mother are also present in procreation
as menstrual blood. Hence:

> Both parties play an important role in procreation, but while fe-
> male's shades feed the foetus with blood in the womb and with milk
> following its birth, the male's *isithunzi* give the child its clan and
> personality characteristics. Through continual deposition of male
> fluid in the womb during pregnancy, a male's shades strengthen
> the unborn child. The work of conception is the work of men. It is
> they, not women, who pass their shades from generation to genera-
> tion. (8)[6]

By Poewe's account, the matrilineal Luapula are rather the mir-
ror image. Here, "female substance is simply the dominant sym-
bol which stands for identification of oneself with others of an
undifferentiated collectivity" (8). There logically follows another
appearance of the "kinship I" (see chapter 1):

> Since clans and tribes are "one person," a person living now is al-
> ways, actually or potentially, the embodiment of someone who lived
> hundreds of years ago. When that person relates the history which
> he inherited with the position, he speaks in the "I" form as if he were
> the ancestor and the events occurred today. Likewise if a prominent
> man married a prominent woman their respective successors and
> whole *clans* many generations thence are transformed into that man
> and woman, are referred to as being that man and woman, and are
> perpetually related as husband and wife, even if the incumbents to
> the two positions are of the same sex. . . . (65; emphasis in original)

---

6. The presence of clan ancestral spirits in semen is also known to the Nyakyusa
(Wilson 1957). As already implied for New Guinea Highland peoples, the collective
clan ancestry may pass to persons by other means besides birth. For Siane, the spirits
of the father's clan can be conveyed by food grown in clan land, by pork, by names, or
by coming into proximity to the flutes that "symbolize" the clan ancestors (Salisbury
1964, 190).

Everything happens here as if the "kinship I," reincarnation, positional succession, common descent, and lineal and affinal relations of procreation were so many aspects of the same thing: mutuality of being, or more particularly its epitome, the union of discrete subjects in the "one person."

By Way of Conclusion

By way of conclusion, some reflections on the cultural variability of the kinship values of birth. For human birth, as has been said, is not a pre-discursive fact. In many lowland South American peoples, it is not necessarily a human birth. Peter Gow writes:

> When a Piro baby is born, the first question asked about it is, "Is it human (*yineru*)?" This question addresses the bodily form of the baby: is it a human, or a fish, or a tortoise, or "an animal nobody had ever seen." The bodily form of the baby is an intrinsic identity form, which is uninfluenced by parental behaviour. (2000, 47; see Taylor 1998 and Vilaça 2002)

Speaking only of human births, we have already seen that the different cultural discourses of procreation are highly variable as concerns the substantive relations of parents and their offspring. There may be no such recognized relations at all (Kamea, Papua New Guinea). Or if there are substance connections set down in procreation, they may be ignored in the way family relations are known (!Kung Bushmen). Then again, only one of the two parents may be substantially linked to the child; either the mother is excluded (Araweté) or the father (Jivaro). If both parents do contribute substance to the fetus, it may be the same substance (Tanimbar) or different substances: and if the latter, these substances may be complementary (Tlingit) or antagonistic (Mae-Enga; Daribi). This is not to mention the great variety of such procreative substances or the intangible contributions of parents such as soul (Tlingit) or breath (China). Then again, the parental bestowals may constitute the child's inner being or outward appearance, and they may entail a collective or an individual identity. Not to mention the important conveyances of spiritual third parties. Should all this cultural variability be laid to a physiological constant? Clearly human birth is a semiotic function of a kinship order, rather than kinship a biological sequitur of birth.

There is, however, one relevant generalization that seems to hold across the several ethnographic references that have been considered here. Either the greater kinship order is already present in persons at birth, as by ancestral means of reproduction; or else kinship relations are largely established in life, as by actual participation in the existence of others. For a given society, these are not necessarily exclusive alternatives, but perhaps only dominant tendencies: the way agnatic clans in the New Guinea Highlands may assimilate some outsiders who have come to live off their lands; or Gê-speaking Amazonians, while generally constructing kinship outside the nuclear family by name-sharing, will observe birth relations within it. But with these reservations, it appears that whether or not kinship is present at procreation depends on the way it is organized in the society at large. Starkly put: kinship is notably built into the relations of procreation in societies predominantly composed of unilineal descent groups; but where cognation or kindred networks prevail, the active participation of people in each other's existence is a more likely means of kin relationships.

A paper by Anne Christine Taylor (1998), in the course of speaking to the relationship between Achuar (Jivaro) personhood and kinship, lays out such alternatives of birth-ascribed and life-achieved kinship in a revelatory manner. The text approaches the issues in two complementary ways: in the beginning, by certain observations on the construction of Jivaro persons, with implications regarding the kinship relations in play; in the end, by observations on the construction of kinship relations, with certain implications regarding personhood.

For the Achuar, the constitution of the person is not given at birth. As just mentioned for Piro people, and as is often the case in Amazonia, there is no assurance *a priori* that the offspring will be human. But if it is, what follows in life is a series of discrete contributions to the composition of the person-body by various members of the society. These "tasks of constitution" are divided among a multitude of contributors:

> . . . from some come the name or successive names, from others this or that substance such as blood or bones, from still others the appearance of that second skin which is ornamentation, and from others finally the faculty of sight, understanding, or speech, or the capacity for heroic action. (1998, 318)

Taylor then draws an explicit contrast to the kind of clanic construction of the fetus that we have seen for Tlingit or Enga. By the multiple endowments on the part of various others, the Jivaro person is referred to the society at large rather than one or another of its segments; "and its body is a palimpsest of the collective existence rather than a part of a mechanism or even the microcosm of an encompassing system." Taylor refuses to speculate whether this ecumenical distribution of person components is a cause or an effect of the prevailing cognatic system—of the kind widely found in the region. But she does say it is at least partly linked to the cognatic order—a kindred schematics, one might note, that usually involves a considerable leeway of kinship choices—by contrast to unilineal structures, which are comparatively rare in lowland South America. Correlatively, this lifetime construction of the person by a multitude of parties is associated with rather vague ideas about the parental contributions to the fetus. The people "seem to accord a very limited interest in the mechanisms of gestation" (320). As we have seen from Taylor's discussion of the same in another context, even when it comes to the father's contribution of semen, this is understood as nourishing the child in the womb rather than substantially composing it; and it is no different from his continuing to establish fatherhood by feeding the child in life. Once again, semen is semiotic, here a food rather than a generative substance.

Taylor notes that "anti-organicism" and "anti-segmentarianism" are found elsewhere in the lowlands, but the Jivaro apparently give these unique twists of pragmatism and individual affect. In a concluding discussion of Jivaro kin relationships, she writes:

> Sociality is not founded on a jural conception of the obligations due to this or that relative: it is rooted rather in the affectivity created by the nature of commensal or intimate relations between individuals. One does not come into the world in an organized society comprised of groups whose members are integrated by virtue of a pre-established etiquette. One is born in a social territory, and in that space everyone constructs his own kinship relations. From the semantic classes appropriate to the system of kin relations that he inherits from his culture, each one forges his own matrix of kin, tracing in quotidian practice his own social network. It is through the exercise of a shared relation that one becomes "husband" or "wife," "father" and "son," and one learns to love his near-ones because they testify to their own affection for him by means of nourishing care—in the same way that one becomes a warrior in response to the hostility of his enemies. (333–34)

Indeed in Amazonia, people both determine their own kin by opposition to their enemies, and they reproduce the former by assimilating the latter. That is another long essay, already written by others, from which, however, the same lesson could be taken: that as constituted from birth to death and even beyond, kinship is culture, all culture. Precisely as Viveiros de Castro wrote of "Amazonian peoples (for example)," the mistake to be avoided is to imagine they entertain some non-standard biological theory of inheritance; whereas, in truth "Amazonian kinship ideas are tantamount to a non-biological theory of life. Kinship here is what you have when you 'do without' a biological theory of relationality" (2009, 241).

Bibliography

Anderson, Margaret Seguin. 2004. "Understanding Tsimshian Potlatch." In *Native Peoples: The Canadian Experience*, 3rd ed., edited
by R. Bruce Morrison and C. Roderick Wilson, 408–30. Don
Millo, Ontario: Oxford University Press.

Aristotle. 2002. *Nicomachean Ethics*. Translated by C. Rowe. New
York: Oxford University Press.

Bamford, Sandra C. 1998. "To Eat for Another: Taboo and the Elici-
tation of Bodily Form among the Kamea of Papua New Guinea."
In *Bodies and Persons: Comparative Perspectives from Africa and
Melanesia*, edited by Michael Lambek and Andrew Strathern,
158–71. Cambridge: Cambridge University Press.

———. 2007. *Biology Unmoored: Melanesian Reflections on Life and
Biotechnology*. Berkeley: University of California Press.

———. 2009. "'Family Trees' among the Kamea of Papua New
Guinea: A Non-Genealogical Approach to Imagining Relatedness." In *Kinship and Beyond: The Genealogical Model Reconsidered*,
edited by Sandra C. Bamford and James Leach, 159–74. New York:
Berghahn.

Bamford, Sandra C., and James Leach, eds. 2009. *Kinship and Beyond:
The Genealogical Model Reconsidered*. New York: Berghahn.

Barnes, Robert H. 1999. "Marriage by Capture." *Journal of the Royal
Anthropological Institute*, n.s., 5: 57–73.

Bastide, R. 1973. "Le principe d'individuation (contribution à une
philosophie africaine)." In *La notion de personne en Afrique Noire*,

Colloque International du Centre National de la Recherche Scientifique 544: 33–43. Paris: Éditions du Centre National de la Recherche Scientifique.

Becker, Anne E. 1995. *Body, Self, and Society: The View from Fiji.* Philadelphia: University of Pennsylvania Press.

Benveniste, Émile. 1971. *Problems in General Linguistics.* Translated by Mary Elizabeth Meek. Coral Gables, FL: University of Miami Press.

Best, Elsdon. 1924. *The Maori.* 2 vols. Wellington, NZ: Harry H. Tombs.

Bloch, Maurice. 1992. *Prey into Hunter: The Politics of Religious Experience.* Cambridge: Cambridge University Press.

Boas, Franz. 1921. *Ethnology of the Kwakiutl,* parts I and II (Annual Report 35). Washington, DC: Bureau of American Ethnology, Smithsonian Institution.

Böck, Monika, and Aparna Rao. 2000. *Culture, Creation, and Procreation: Concepts of Kinship in South Asian Practice.* New York: Berghahn.

Bodenhorn, Barbara. 2000. "He Used to Be My Relative: Exploring the Bases of Relatedness among Iñupiat of Northern Alaska." In *Cultures of Relatedness: New Approaches to the Study of Kinship,* edited by Janet Carsten, 128–48. Cambridge: Cambridge University Press.

Busby, Cecilia. 1997. "Of Marriage and Marriageability: Gender and Dravidian Kinship." *Journal of the Royal Anthropological Institute* 3: 21–42.

Carsten, Janet. 2000a. Introduction to *Cultures of Relatedness: New Approaches to the Study of Kinship,* edited by Janet Carsten, 1–36. Cambridge: Cambridge University Press.

———, ed. 2000b. *Cultures of Relatedness: New Approaches to the Study of Kinship.* Cambridge: Cambridge University Press.

———. 2004. *After Kinship.* Cambridge: Cambridge University Press.

Charles-Edwards, Thomas M. 1993. *Early Irish and Welsh Kinship.* Oxford: Clarendon Press.

Chun, Allen J. 1990. "Conceptions of Kinship and Kingship in Classical Chou China." *Tsung Pao* 56: 16–48.

Clunas, Craig. 2004. *Elegant Debts: The Social Art of Wei Zhengming.* Honolulu: University of Hawai'i Press.

Clunie, Fergus. 1977. *Fijian Weapons and Warfare* (Bulletin of the Fiji Museum 2). Suva: Fiji Museum.

Da Matta, Roberto. 1982. *A Divided World: Apinayé Social Structure.*
Cambridge, MA: Harvard University Press.

Davis, Kingsley, and W. Lloyd Warner. 1937. "Structural Analysis of
Kinship." *American Anthropologist* 39: 291–313.

Derlon, Brigitte. 1998. "Corps, cosmos et société en Nouvelle-Irlande."
In *La production du corps: Approches anthropologiques et historiques*,
edited by Maurice Godelier and Michel Panoff, 163–86. Amsterdam: Éditions des archives contemporaines.

Descola, Philippe. 1996. *The Spears of Twilight: Life and Death in the
Amazonian Jungle.* New York: New Press.

Dillon, John, and Tania Gergel, eds. 2003. *The Greek Sophists.* London:
Penguin.

Downs, Richard E. 1956. *The Religion of the Bare'e-Speaking Toradja of
Central Celebes.* The Hague: Uitgeverij Excelsior.

Dumont, Louis. 1953. "The Dravidian Kinship Terminology as an
Expression of Marriage." *Man*, o.s., 53: 34–39.

————. 1963. *Affinity as a Value: Marriage Alliance in South India with
Comparative Essays on Australia.* Chicago: University of Chicago
Press.

Durkheim, Émile. 1898. Review of *Zur Urgeschichte der Ehe: Totem-
ismus, Gruppenehe, Mutterecht*, by J. Kohler. *L'Année Sociologique* 1:
306–19.

Edwards, Jeanette, and Marilyn Strathern. 2000. "Including Your
Own." In *Cultures of Relatedness: New Approaches to the Study of
Kinship*, edited by Janet Carsten, 149–66. Cambridge: Cambridge
University Press.

Faubion, James D. 2001. Introduction to *The Ethics of Kinship: Ethnographic Inquiries*, edited by James Faubion, 1–28. London: Rowman
& Littlefield.

Fausto, Carlos. 2007. "Feasting on People." *Current Anthropology* 44:
497–514, 521–24.

Feinberg, Richard. 1981. "The Meaning of 'Sibling' on Anuta Island."
In *Siblingship in Oceania: Studies in the Meaning of Kin Relations*,
edited by Mac Marshall, 105–48. ASAO Monographs, No. 5. Ann
Arbor: University of Michigan Press.

Forman, Shepard. 1980. "Descent, Alliance, and Exchange Ideology
among the Makassae of Timor." In *The Flow of Life: Essays on
Eastern Indonesia*, edited by James J. Fox, 152–77. Cambridge, MA:
Harvard University Press.

Fortes, Meyer. 1969. *Kinship and the Social Order*. Chicago: Aldine.

Foster, Robert J. 1990. "Nurture and Force-Feeding: Mortuary Feasting and the Construction of Collective Individuals in a New Ireland Society." *American Ethnologist* 17: 431–48.

Fox, James J., ed. 1980. *The Flow of Life: Essays on Eastern Indonesia*. Cambridge, MA: Harvard University Press.

Franklin, Sarah, and Susan McKinnon, eds. 2001. *Relative Values: Reconfiguring Kinship Studies*. Durham, NC: Duke University Press.

Geertz, Hildred, and Clifford Geertz. 1975. *Kinship in Bali*. Chicago: University of Chicago Press.

Gell, Alfred. 1998. *Art and Agency: An Anthropological Theory*. Oxford: Clarendon Press.

Gellner, E. 1960. "The Concept of Kinship." *Philosophy of Science* 27: 187–204.

Gewertz, Deborah B. 1984. "The Tchambuli View of Persons: A Critique of Individualism in the Works of Mead and Chodorow." *American Anthropologist* 86: 615–29.

Glasse, R. M. 1969. "Marriage in South Fore." In *Pigs, Pearshells, and Women: Marriage in the New Guinea Highlands*, edited by R. M. Glasse and M. J. Meggitt, 16–37. Englewood Cliffs, NJ: Prentice-Hall.

Godelier, Maurice. 1998. "Corps, parenté, pouvoir(s) chez les Baruya de Nouvelle-Guinée." In *La production du corps: Approches anthropologiques et historiques*, edited by Maurice Godelier and Michel Panoff, 1–38. Amsterdam: Éditions des archives contemporaines.

Godelier, Maurice, and Michel Panoff. 1998. Introduction to *La production du corps: Approches anthropologiques et historiques*, edited by Maurice Godelier and Michel Panoff, xi–xxv. Amsterdam: Éditions des archives contemporaines.

Goodale, Jane. 1981. "Siblings as Spouses: The Reproduction and Replacement of Kaulong Society." In *Siblingship in Oceania: Studies in the Meaning of Kin Relations*, edited by Mac Marshall, 277–305. Ann Arbor: University of Michigan Press.

Gow, Peter. 1991. *Of Mixed Blood: Kinship and History in Peruvian Amazonia*. Oxford: Clarendon Press.

———. 2000. "Helpless: The Affective Preconditions of Piro Social Life." In *The Anthropology of Love and Anger: The Aesthetics of Conviviality in Native Amazonia*, edited by Joanna Overing and Alan Passes, 46–63. London: Routledge.

Gregory, Christopher A. 1982. *Gifts and Commodities*. London: Clarendon Press.

Guemple, D. L. 1965. "Saunik: Name Sharing as a Factor Governing Eskimo Kinship Terms." *Ethnology* 4: 323–35.

Harrison, Simon. 1990. *Stealing People's Names: History and Politics in a Sepik River Cosmology*. Cambridge: Cambridge University Press.

Hess, Sabine C. 2009. *Person and Place: Ideals and the Practice of Sociality on Vanua Lava, Vanuatu*. London: Berghahn.

Hocart, A. M. 1915. "Chieftainship and the Sister's Son in the Pacific." *American Anthropologist* 17: 631–43.

———. 1970. *The Life-Giving Myth and Other Essays*. London: Tavistock & Methuen.

Hornborg, Alf. 1988. *Dualism and Hierarchy in Lowland South America: Trajectories of Indigenous Social Organization*. Uppsala: Almqvist & Wiksell.

Huntsman, Judith. 1981. "Complementary and Similar Kinsmen in Tokelau." In *Siblingship in Oceania: Studies in the Meaning of Kin Relations*, edited by Mac Marshall, 79–103. Ann Arbor: University of Michigan Press.

Jensen, Keith, Josep Call, and Michael Tomasello. 2007. "Chimpanzees Are Rational Maximizers in an Ultimate Game." *Science* 318: 107–9.

Jensen, Keith, Brian Hare, Josep Call, and Michael Tomasello. 2006. "What's in It for Me?: Self-Regard Precludes Altruism and Spite in Chimpanzees." *Royal Society, Proceedings: Biological Sciences* 273: 1013–21.

Johansen, Jørgen Prytz. 1954. *The Maori and His Religion*. Copenhagen: Munksgaard.

Jolly, Margaret. 1981. "People and Their Products in South Pentecost." In *Vanuatu: Politics, Economics and Ritual in Island Melanesia*, edited by Michael Allen, 269–93. Sydney: Academic Press.

———. 1994. *Women of the Place: Kastom, Colonialism, and Gender in Vanuatu*. Chur, Switzerland: Harwood.

Kahn, Charles H. 1994. *Anaximander and the Origins of Greek Cosmology*. Indianapolis: Hackett.

Kan, Sergei. 1986. "The 19th-Century Tlingit Potlatch: A New Perspective." *American Ethnologist* 13: 191–212.

———. 1989. *Symbolic Immortality: Tlingit Potlatch in the Nineteenth Century*. Washington, DC: Smithsonian Institution Press.

Kant, Immanuel. 1950. *Prolegomena to Any Future Metaphysics*. New York: Macmillan.

Krige, Eileen J., and Jacob D. Krige. 1943. *The Realm of a Rain Queen: A Study of the Pattern of Lovedu Society*. London: Oxford University Press for the International African Institute.

Kuper, Adam. 1999. *Culture: The Anthropologists' Account*. Cambridge, MA: Harvard University Press.

LaFontaine, Jean. 1973. "Descent in New Guinea: An Africanist View." In *The Character of Kinship*, edited by Jack Goody, 35–52. Cambridge: Cambridge University Press.

Landes, Ruth. 1969. *Ojibwa Sociology*. New York: AMS Press [Reproduced from the 1937 edition, Columbia University Press].

Lave, Jean, Alex Stepick, and Lee Sailer. 1977. "Extending the Scope of Formal Semantic Analysis: A Technique for Integration Analysis of Kinship Relations with Analyses of Other Dyadic Relations." *American Ethnologist* 4: 321–37.

Leach, Edmund R. 1961a. *Pul Eliya, a Village in Ceylon: A Study in Land Tenure and Kinship*. Cambridge: Cambridge University Press.

———. 1961b. *Rethinking Anthropology*. London: Robert Cunningham & Sons.

———. 1962. "Concerning Trobriand Clans and the Kinship Category 'Tabu.'" In *The Developmental Cycle in Domestic Groups*, edited by Jack Goody, 120–45. Cambridge: Cambridge University Press.

Leach, James. 2003. *Creative Land: Place and Procreation on the Rai Coast of Papua New Guinea*. New York: Berghahn.

Leenhardt, Maurice. 1949. Préface to *Les carnets de Lucien Lévy-Bruhl*, by Lucien Lévy-Bruhl, v–xxi. Paris: Presses Universitaires de France.

———. 1979. *Do Kamo*. Chicago: University of Chicago Press.

Lévi-Strauss, Claude. 1964. *Structural Anthropology*. New York: Basic Books.

———. 1969. *The Elementary Structures of Kinship*. Boston: Beacon.

Lévy-Bruhl, Lucien. 1949. *Les carnets de Lucien Lévy-Bruhl*. Paris: Presses Universitaires de France.

———. 1985. *How Natives Think*. Princeton, NJ: Princeton University Press.

Lewis, Gilbert. 1980. *Day of Shining Red*. Cambridge: Cambridge University Press.

Lieber, Michael D. 1990. "Lamarkian Definitions of Identity on Kpingamarangi and Pohnpei." In *Cultural Identity and Ethnicity in the Pacific*, edited by Jocelyn Linnekin and Lin Poyer, 71–101. Honolulu: University of Hawai'i Press.

LiPuma, Edward. 1988. *The Gift of Kinship: Structure and Practice in Maring Social Organization.* Cambridge: Cambridge University Press.

Maning, Frederick E. 1922. *Old New Zealand . . . by a Pakeha Maori.* Auckland: Whitcombe & Tombs.

Marriott, McKim. 1976. "Hindu Transactions: Diversity without Dualism." In *Transaction and Meaning: Directions in the Anthropology of Exchange and Symbolic Behavior*, edited by Bruce Kapferer, 109–42. Philadelphia: ISHI Publications.

Marshall, Lorna. 1957. "The Kin Terminology of the !Kung Bushmen." *Africa* 27: 1–25.

Marshall, Mac. 1977. "The Nature of Nurture." *American Ethnologist* 4: 643–62.

Marx, Karl. 1973. *Grundrisse: Foundations of the Critique of Political Economy.* Edited and translated by Martin Nicolaus. Harmondsworth, UK: Penguin.

McKinley, Robert. 1981. "Cain and Abel on the Malay Peninsula." In *Siblingship in Oceania: Studies in the Meaning of Kin Relations*, edited by Mac Marshall, 335–418. Ann Arbor: University of Michigan Press.

————. 2001. "The Philosophy of Kinship: A Reply to Schneider's Critique of the Study of Kinship." In *The Cultural Analysis of Kinship: The Legacy of David M. Schneider*, edited by Richard Feinberg and Martin Oppenheimer, 131–67. Urbana: University of Illinois Press.

McKinnon, Susan. 1991. *From a Shattered Sun: Hierarchy, Gender, and Alliance in the Tanimbar Islands.* Madison: University of Wisconsin Press.

————. 2006. *Neo-Liberal Genetics: The Myths and Moral Tales of Evolutionary Psychology.* Chicago: Prickly Paradigm.

Mead, Margaret. 1935. *Sex and Temperament in Three Primitive Societies.* New York: Morrow.

Meggitt, Mervyn. 1965. *The Lineage System of the Mae-Enga.* Edinburgh: Oliver and Boyd.

Melatti, Julio Cezar. 1979. "The Relationship System of the Krahó." In *Dialectical Societies: The Gê and Bororo of Central Brazil*, edited by

David Maybury Lewis, 46–79. Cambridge, MA: Harvard University Press.

Merlan, Francesca, and Alan Rumsey. 1991. *Ku Waru: Language and Segmentary Politics in the Western Nebilyer Valley, Papua New Guinea.* Cambridge: Cambridge University Press.

Meskell, Lynn, and Rosemary A. Joyce. 2003. *Embodied Lives: Figuring Ancient Maya and Egyptian Experience.* London: Routledge.

Middleton, Karen. 2000. "How Karembola Men Become Mothers." In *Cultures of Relatedness: New Approaches to the Study of Kinship*, edited by Janet Carsten, 104–27. Cambridge: Cambridge University Press.

Morgan, Lewis Henry. 1871. *Systems of Consanguinity and Affinity in the Human Family.* In *Smithsonian Contributions to Knowledge*, vol. 17. Washington, DC: Smithsonian Institution.

Mosko, Mark S. 1992. "Motherless Sons: 'Divine Kings' and 'Partible Persons' in Melanesia and Polynesia." *Man*, n.s., 27: 697–717.

———. 2010. "Partible Penitents: Dividual Personhood and Christian Practices in Melanesia and the West." *Journal of the Royal Anthropological Institute*, n.s., 16: 215–40.

Munn, Nancy D. 1986. *The Fame of Gawa: A Symbolic Study of Value Transformation in a Massim (Papua New Guinea) Society.* Cambridge: Cambridge University Press.

Nuttal, Mark. 2000. "Choosing Kin: Sharing and Subsistence in a Greenlander Hunting Community." In *Dividends of Kinship: Meanings and Uses of Social Relatedness*, edited by Peter P. Schweitzer, 33–60. London: Routledge.

Parkin, Robert. 1996. "Genealogy and Category: An Operational View." *L'Homme* 36 (139): 87–108.

Pitt-Rivers, Julian. 1973. "Kith and Kin." In *The Character of Kinship*, edited by Jack Goody, 89–105. Cambridge: Cambridge University Press.

Poewe, Karla. 1981. *Matrilineal Ideology: Male–Female Dynamics in Luapula, Zambia.* London: Academic Press for the International African Institute.

Radcliffe-Brown, A. R. 1924. "The Mother's Brother in South Africa." *South African Journal of Science* 21: 542–55.

Read, Kenneth E. 1955. "Morality and the Concept of the Person among the Gahuku-Gama." *Oceania* 24: 233–82.

Ricoeur, Paul. 1979. "The Model of the Text: Meaningful Action

Considered as a Text." In *Interpretive Social Science: A Reader*, edited by Paul Rabinow and William M. Sullivan, 73–101. Berkeley: University of California Press.

Rival, Laura. 1998. "Androgynous Parents and Guest Children: The Huaorani Couvade." *Journal of the Royal Anthropological Institute* 4: 619–42.

Rosaldo, Renato. 1980. *Ilongot Headhunting, 1883–1974: A Study in Society and History*. Stanford, CA: Stanford University Press.

Rubenstein, Robert. 1981. "Siblings in Malo Culture." In *Siblingship in Oceania: Studies in the Meaning of Kin Relations*, edited by Mac Marshall, 307–34. Ann Arbor: University of Michigan Press.

Rumsey, Alan. 2000. "Agency, Personhood and the 'I' of Discourse in the Pacific and Beyond." *Journal of the Royal Anthropological Institute*, n.s., 6: 101–15.

Sahlins, Marshall. 1962. *Moala: Culture and Nature on a Fijian Island*. Ann Arbor: University of Michigan Press.

———. 1981. "The Stranger-King; or Dumézil among the Fijians." *Journal of Pacific History* 16: 107–32.

———. 2000. *Culture in Practice: Selected Essays*. New York: Zone.

———. 2004. *Apologies to Thucydides: Understanding History and Culture and Vice Versa*. Chicago: University of Chicago Press.

———. 2008. *The Western Illusion of Human Nature*. Chicago: Prickly Paradigm.

———. 2010. "The Whole Is a Part: Intercultural Politics of Order and Change." In *Experiments in Holism: Theory and Practice in Contemporary Anthropology*, edited by Ton Otto and Nils Bubandt, 102–26. Oxford: Wiley-Blackwell.

———. 2011. "What Kinship Is." *Journal of the Royal Anthropological Institute*, n.s., 17: 2–19, 227–42.

Salisbury, R. F. 1964. "New Guinea Highland Models and Descent Theory." *Man*, o.s., 64: 168–71.

Sather, Clifford. 1993. "The One-Sided One: Iban Rice Myths, Agricultural Ritual and Notions of Ancestry." *Contributions to Southeast Asian Ethnography* 10: 119–47.

Scheffler, Harold W. 1976. "The Meaning of Kinship in American Culture: Another View." In *Meaning in Anthropology*, edited by Keith Basso and Henry Selby. Albuquerque: University of New Mexico Press.

Scheffler, Harold W., and Floyd G. Lounsbury. 1971. *A Study in*

Structural Semantics: The Siriono Kinship System. Englewood Cliffs, NJ: Prentice-Hall.

Schneider, David M. 1968. *American Kinship: A Cultural Account*. Englewood Cliffs, NJ: Prentice-Hall.

———. 1972. "What Is Kinship All About?" In *Kinship Studies in the Morgan Centennial Year*, edited by Priscilla Reining, 32–63. Washington, DC: Anthropological Society of Washington DC.

———. 1977. "Kinship, Nationality and Religion in American Culture: Towards a Definition of Kinship." In *Symbolic Anthropology: A Reader in the Study of Symbols and Meanings*, edited by Janet L. Dolgin, David S. Kemnitzer, and David Schneider, 63–71. New York: Columbia University Press.

———. 1980. *American Kinship: A Cultural Account*. 2nd ed. Chicago: University of Chicago Press.

———. 1984. *A Critique of the Study of Kinship*. Ann Arbor: University of Michigan Press.

Schrauwers, Albert. 1999. "Negotiating Parentage: The Political Economy of 'Kinship' in Central Sulawesi." *American Ethnologist* 26: 310–23.

Seeger, Anthony. 1981. *Nature and Society in Central Brazil: The Suya Indians of the Mato Grosso*. Cambridge, MA: Harvard University Press.

Smith, DeVerne Reed. 1981. "Palauan Siblingship: A Study in Structural Complementarity." In *Siblingship in Oceania: Studies in the Meaning of Kin Relations*, edited by Mac Marshall, 225–73. Ann Arbor: University of Michigan Press.

Stasch, Rupert. 2009. *Society of Others: Kinship and Mourning in a West Papuan Place*. Berkeley: University of California Press.

Strathern, Andrew. 1973. "Kinship, Descent and Locality: Some New Guinea Examples." In *The Character of Kinship*, edited by Jack Goody, 21–34. Cambridge: Cambridge University Press.

Strathern, Marilyn. 1988. *The Gender of the Gift: Problems with Women and Problems with Society in Melanesia*. Berkeley: University of California Press.

———. 1992. *Reproducing the Future: Anthropology, Kinship, and the New Reproductive Technologies*. New York: Routledge.

Taylor, Anne Christine. 1996. "The Soul's Body and Its States: An Amazonian Perspective on the Nature of Being Human." *Journal of the Royal Anthropological Institute*, n.s., 2: 201–15.

————. 1998. "Corps immortels, devoir d'oublie: Formes humaines et trajectoires de vie chez les Achuar." In *La production du corps: Approches anthropologiques et historiques*, edited by Maurice Godelier and Michel Panoff, 317–38. Amsterdam: Éditions des archives contemporaines.

————. 2000. "Le sexe de la proie: Représentations Jivaro du lien de parenté." *L'Homme*, nos. 154–55: 309–33.

Tomasello, Michael. 1999a. *The Cultural Origins of Human Cognition.* Cambridge, MA: Harvard University Press.

————. 1999b. "The Human Adaptation for Culture." *Annual Review of Anthropology* 28: 509–29.

————. 2006. "Why Don't Apes Point?" In *Roots of Human Sociality: Culture, Cognition and Interaction*, edited by N. J. Enfield and S. C. Levinson, 506–24. Oxford: Berg.

————. 2008. *Origins of Human Communication.* Cambridge, MA: MIT Press.

————. 2009. *Why We Cooperate.* Cambridge, MA: MIT Press.

Tomasello, Michael, Malinda Carpenter, Josep Call, Tanya Behne, and Henrike Moll. 2005. "Understanding and Sharing Intentions: The Origins of Cultural Cognition." *Behavioral and Brain Sciences* 28: 675–735.

Tomasello, Michael, Malinda Carpenter, and R. Peter Hobson. 2005. *The Emergence of Social Cognition in Three Young Chimpanzees.* Boston: Blackwell.

Tomasello, Michael, Anne Kruger, and Hilary Horn Ratner. 1993. "Cultural Learning." *Behavioral and Brain Sciences* 16: 495–552.

Traube, Elizabeth. 1986. *Cosmology and Social Life: Ritual Exchange among the Mambai of East Timor.* Chicago: University of Chicago Press.

Trevarthen, Colwyn, and Kenneth J. Aitkin. 2001. "Infant Intersubjectivity." *Journal of Child Psychology and Psychiatry* 42: 3–48.

Turner, Victor. 1957. *Schism and Continuity in an African Society: A Study in Ndembu Village Life.* Manchester: University Press on behalf of the Rhodes-Livingstone Institute, Northern Rhodesia.

Tylor, Edward B. 1865. *Researches into the Early History of Mankind and the Development of Civilization.* 1st ed. London: J. Murray.

————. 1878. *Researches into the Early History of Mankind and the Development of Civilization.* 3rd ed. London: J. Murray.

Urban, Greg. 1989. "The 'I' of Discourse." In *Semiotics, Self and Society,* edited by Benjamin Lee and Greg Urban, 27–51. Berlin: Mouton de Gruyter.

Vilaça, Aparecida. 2002. "Making Kin Out of Others in Amazonia." *Journal of the Royal Anthropological Institute*, n.s., 8: 347–65.

————. 2005. "Chronically Unstable Bodies: Reflections on Amazonian Corporalities." *Journal of the Royal Anthropological Institute*, n.s., 11: 445–64.

————. 2010. *Strange Enemies: Indigenous Agency and Scenes of Encounters in Amazonia*. Durham, NC: Duke University Press.

Viveiros de Castro, Eduardo. 1992. *From the Enemy's Point of View: Humanity and Divinity in an Amazonian Society*. Chicago: University of Chicago Press.

————. 2004. "Perspectival Anthropology and the Method of Controlled Comparison." *Tipití* 2: 3–22.

————. 2009. "The Gift and the Given: Three Nano-Essays on Kinship and Magic." In *Kinship and Beyond: The Genealogical Model Reconsidered*, edited by Sandra C. Bamford and James Leach, 237–68. New York: Berghahn.

Wagner, Roy. 1977. "Analogic Kinship: A Daribi Example." *American Ethnologist* 4: 623–42.

Wouden, Franciscus A. van. 1968. *Types of Social Structure in Eastern Indonesia*. The Hague: Martinus Nijhoff.

White, Leslie. 1949. *The Science of Culture: A Study of Man and Civilization*. New York: Farrar Straus.

Wilson, Monica H. 1950. "Nyakyusa Kinship." In *African Systems of Kinship and Marriage*, edited by A. R. Radcliffe-Brown and Cyril Daryll Forde, 111–39. London: Oxford University Press for the International African Institute.

————. 1951. *Good Company: A Study of Nyakyusa Age-Villages*. London: Oxford University Press for the International African Institute.

————. 1957. *Rituals of Kinship among the Nyakyusa*. London: Oxford University Press for the International African Institute.

————. 1959. *Communal Rituals of the Nyakyusa*. London: Oxford University Press for the International African Institute.

Index